Spirituality, Justice, and Pedagogy

Edited by David I. Smith, John Shortt,
and John Sullivan

The Stapleford Centre
Nottingham, UK
2006

A Special Issue of
The Journal of Education & Christian Belief
Volume 10:2 (Autumn 2006)

The Stapleford Centre

The Old Lace Mill
Frederick Road,
Stapleford,
Nottingham
NG9 8FN
UK

This themed issue of the Journal of Education and Christian Belief is published in cooperation with the Association of Christian Teachers (Hertfordshire, UK) and the Kuyers Institute for Christian Teaching and Learning (Grand Rapids, MI, USA).

British Library Cataloguing in Publication Data
A catalogue record for this book is available from the British Library.

ISBN-13: 978-1-902234-43-4
ISBN-10: 1-902234-43-X
ISSN: 1366-5456

Typeset by Toucan Design, Exeter, Devon, and printed in the USA for the Stapleford Centre by Color House Graphics, Grand Rapids, MI.

JE&CB 10:2 (2006) 1–168   1366-5456

Contents

Contributors

- **Doug Blomberg** is Senior Member in Philosophy of Education at the Institute for Christian Studies, Toronto, Canada. He is the author of *Wisdom and Curriculum: Christian Schooling After Postmodernity*, to be published by Dordt College Press.

- **Chris Elisara** is the founder and executive director of the Creation Care Study Program in Belize. A native New Zealander, his Ph.D. in cross-cultural education was earned at Biola University, California, USA.

- **Philip Fountain** was Program Director of CCSP Belize from 2003 to 2005. He is currently carrying out doctoral research on the intersections between religion and international aid and development at Australian National University, Canberra, Australia.

- **Brad Hadaway** is Associate Professor of Philosophy and Director of the Oxford Programs at Georgetown College, Georgetown, Kentucky, USA.

- **Louis Gallien** is Distinguished Professor of Education at Regent Graduate School of Education. He has just completed a book for Teachers College Press on academic achievement among African-American college students. He received the Chancellor's Award in 2006 as Professor of the Year at Regent University, Virginia Beach/Alexandria, Virginia, USA.

- **LaTrelle Jackson** is Associate Professor of Psychology and Director of the Psychological Services Clinic at the School of Psychology and Counseling at Regent University, Virginia Beach/Alexandria, Virginia, USA.

- **Glenn E. Sanders** is Professor of History and Chair of the Divisional of Behavioral and Social Sciences, Oklahoma Baptist University, Shawnee, Oklahoma, USA. His professional interests include the teaching of history, the relationships between Christian faith and learning in colleges and universities, and Muslim-Christian relations.

- **John Shortt** is Travelling Secretary for European Educators' Christian Association (EurECA) and an educational consultant based in Leighton Buzzard, UK.

- **David I. Smith** is Associate Professor of German and Director of the Kuyers Institute for Christian Teaching and Learning at Calvin College in Grand Rapids, Michigan, USA.

- **John Sullivan** is Professor of Christian Education at Liverpool Hope University, Liverpool, UK. He has a particular interest in Christian educational leadership and has published widely on religion and education.

- **Steve VanderLeest** is Professor of Engineering at Calvin College in Grand Rapids, Michigan, USA, and was also recently appointed chair of his department.

- **Nicholas Wolterstorff** is Noah Porter Professor Emeritus of Philosophical Theology at Yale University, New Haven, Connecticut, USA, and Senior Fellow at the Institute for Advanced Studies in Culture, University of Virginia. He has written books on metaphysics, aesthetics, political philosophy, epistemology and theology, philosophy of religion, and education.

JE&CB 10:2 (2006) 7–21   1366-5456

David I. Smith, John Sullivan, and John Shortt

Introduction: Connecting Spirituality, Justice, and Pedagogy

"Those who are into spirituality are usually not into justice and those who are into justice are usually not into spirituality."[1] This comment was made by Nicholas Wolterstorff during his plenary address to the recent conference "Spirituality, Justice, and Pedagogy," sponsored by the Kuyers Institute for Christian Teaching and Learning, from which the papers in this volume (including that plenary address) are drawn. A similar suspicion lay behind the conception of the conference. There is voluminous discussion of spirituality in education these days, running the full gamut from plans for explicit faith formation through efforts at a mediating "phenomenology of the distinctively human"[2] to maximally generic ideas of spirituality as a "heightening of awareness" and the like.[3] There is also a wide literature discussing educational justice, attending to matters such as discrimination and representation in relation to various aspects of personal identity and the ways in which educational provision and educational assumptions follow the paths of social privilege. An important area of intersection between these discussions does exist (see, for instance, the recent writing of David Purpel[4]), but nevertheless a common pattern is for writings concerned with educational justice to treat faith and spirituality with indifference, or even hostility, and for writings on spirituality in education to focus on inner realities to the exclusion of the social, and even sometimes the ethical.[5] These two tendencies, of course, easily become mutually reinforcing. The aim of this volume, and of the conference that gave rise to it, has been to resist the dichotomy and explore places where spirituality, justice, and pedagogy might constructively interact, with a particular focus on Christian spirituality.

Both the above comments and Wolterstorff's talk of what is "usually" the case point to the existence of exceptions. There have indeed always been exceptions; brief exploration of a few examples from the history of Christian reflection on education may help to set the stage for the contemporary reflections in the essays that follow and to set aside any impression that the conjunction of themes explored in them is radically new.

Comenius and the Garden of Delight

Consider first John Amos Comenius, one of the most significant figures in the history of Western education and a Moravian bishop. His 17th-century writings had a long-term influence on Western schooling, and his textbooks were used by children for two centuries after his death. One of the things for which he is most commonly remembered is his commitment to universal education. Comenius argued that education had to be provided in common to both rich and poor, to those of both greater and lesser intellectual ability, and to both boys and girls, lest false distinctions of worth between these groups should lead to pride.[6] His educational program was explicitly grounded in "the expressed wish…for full power of development into full humanity not of one particular person, but of *every single individual*, young and old, rich and poor, noble and ignoble, men and women – in a word, every being born on earth, with the ultimate aim of providing education to the entire human race regardless of age, class, sex and nationality."[7] This opposition to prejudicial treatment extended to his pedagogical goals, as he argued that "[b]ias towards persons, nations, languages and religious sects must be totally eliminated if we are to prevent love or hatred, envy or contempt, or any other emotion from interfering with our plans for happiness…."[8] It is also reflected in the content of his school textbooks. His famous language textbook, the *Orbis Pictus*, includes a chapter on the virtue of justice, admonishing students not only that there is a sword of retribution "to punish and restrain evil men," but that they should "stand to their covenants and promises" and "deal candidly" with their neighbor.[9]

These emphases in Comenius are explicitly grounded in his theology. He saw the need for universal education as grounded in the creation of each individual in the image of God. God "has frequently asserted that with Him there is no respect of persons" and "wishes to be acknowledged, to be loved, and to be praised by all upon whom He has impressed his image" – accordingly, to treat any individual injuriously, or to deny them the benefits of education, is to "commit an injury not only against those who share the same nature as ourselves, but against God Himself."[10] The existence of each individual as a being with spiritual needs, worth, and potential left no room, he argued, for arbitrary exclusion of some learners: "There is no exemption from human education except for non-humans."[11]

A second important thread in his thinking, not only linking theology, justice, and education, but also connecting these to the desired outcomes of educational formation, is his central use of the image of the "garden of delight" as a normative image for schools, classrooms, and individuals. This image is drawn in the first place from the creation story in Genesis 1, where the description of the "garden of delight" (a translation of the more familiar phrase "garden of Eden") gave rise to a long tradition of associating that image with teaching and with spiritual formation – the individual was not only created to *indwell* a garden of delight, but to *become* one by being made just through cultivation by God.[12] The image is also mediated through the Old Testament prophets, where the idea of the community as a garden of delight is bound up with matters of justice, as when the Israelite community is spoken of as a vineyard in Isaiah 5:

> The vineyard of the Lord Almighty
> is the house of Israel,
> and the men of Judah
> are the garden of his delight.
> And he looked for justice, but saw bloodshed;
> for righteousness, but heard cries of distress.
> (v. 7 NIV)

The garden of delight thus does not represent a mere nostalgia for origins, but rather an eschatological horizon of possibility to which schooling is to be held accountable.

This yoking of justice and delight with spiritual growth is reflected at many points in Comenius' educational writings. He describes the purpose of human existence as being "that we may serve God, his creatures and ourselves, and that we may enjoy the pleasure to be derived from God, from his creatures and from ourselves."[13] Schooling is to pursue this threefold service and delight as its goal. Pleasure in self is defined as "that very sweet delight which arises when a man, who is given over to virtue, rejoices in his own honest disposition, since he sees himself prompt to all things which the order of justice requires."[14] This definition both draws virtue into close contact with Comenius' view of piety as delight in God's goodness, and points spiritual growth beyond the individual's inner life. Youth must be taught from the beginning, he urges, "that we are born not for ourselves alone, but for God and for our neighbour, that is to say, for the human race."[15] Comenius goes further: the end of education should be that "the entire world should be a garden of delight for God, for people, and for things"[16] Spirituality, pedagogy, and social and environmental well-being are drawn together in Comenius' theologically rooted vision of the high calling placed upon educators.

Freire, Easter, and Resurrection

Turning to a different time, a different place, and a different, more politically radical vision of education, the work of the celebrated Brazilian educator Paulo Freire likewise exhibits connections between a vision for social justice, a concern for educational reform, and roots in Christian spiritual concerns. Freire is widely known for his focus on developing a pedagogy with and among the oppressed that would avoid transmitting to them and reproducing the social conditions of their oppression. Instead, Freire worked towards a "conscientization" that takes shape in a combination of critical awareness of social injustices and concrete action toward their removal.[17] He sought a pedagogy in which learners would be able to become conscious subjects and agents, rather than passive objects and recipients of static pictures of reality.

Freire's passionate calls to commitment to the oppressed in Latin America and elsewhere combine the Marxist language of dialectic and revolution with the language of hope, love, and the heart, and his work has overt connections with Catholic Christianity and liberation theology. While harshly critical of the socially conservative role of particular churches and of any spirituality that would divorce the inner and the transcendent from concrete involvement in history and concrete identification with human suffering, Freire maintained that "the original Christian position is itself prophetic, at whatever point in time and place"[18] and wrote of the need for a "real Easter" that would not be "commemorative rhetoric" but rather, through the pursuit of liberation of the oppressed, "the death which makes life possible."[19] This life-bringing resurrection stands opposed to "the lust to possess" that substitutes having for being and treats people as objects.[20] Freire's emphasis on a humanizing pedagogy is explained by him as reflecting our relationship with our Creator, which is not one of dominance but rather one in which "humans have their return to their Source, Who liberates them."[21] On a more personal note, Freire wrote of "the fundamental importance of my faith in my struggle for overcoming an oppressive reality and for building a less ugly society, one that is less evil and more humane. All arguments in favor of the legitimacy of my struggle for a more people-oriented society have their deepest roots in my faith."[22] Here again, in a different idiom, a different branch of the Christian church (Comenius led the United Brethren, Freire's roots were Roman Catholic), and with a different political vision of justice, we find spirituality, justice, and pedagogy coming together in a fertile mix.

Trends in Catholic Education

Connections between spirituality, justice, and pedagogy have also been reflected in much Catholic reflection on education in recent decades. In parallel with increasing social integration of Catholics, Popes, beginning with Leo XIII in the 1890s, issued statements about social matters, with implications for the involvement of Catholics in society. The Second Vatican Council (1962-65) was the most significant event that moved Catholics from being an inward-looking community, focused on a vertical relationship between God and the soul as central to the life of faith, to being a community with a concomitant horizontal dimension. Since love of God must be demonstrated by love of neighbor, participation in the world became the order of the day. The windows of the church were thrown open, dialogue and cooperation with people of all faiths and none became an imperative. Soon afterwards, in various major meetings of the bishops, promotion of justice and peace came to be treated as constitutive elements in communicating the Gospel. Catholic teaching during the past forty years has become increasingly saturated with such themes as justice, the common good, human dignity, solidarity, subsidiarity, recognition of the relative or derived autonomy of the secular order, stewardship, human rights, and liberation from all that prevents human flourishing. Spirituality, far from being other-worldly in orientation, became world-affirming and a spur to political action on behalf of the needy. In political theology, Johann Baptist Metz and in liberation theology, Gustavo Gutierrez became influential figures in Catholic theology, taking much further than had their predecessors, Jacques Maritain and Karl Rahner, the implications of Christian faith for social involvement and critique.[23]

It followed, from this shift in church teaching, that Catholic education should give more explicit attention to education for social engagement as an integral part of the duties of disciples, and that spirituality should embrace a concern for justice.[24] Many new resources for Catholic schools have become available that summarize, explain, and explore the ramifications of Catholic social teaching.[25]

Thomas Groome has been an influential contributor to this stream of Catholic educational thought.[26] Groome, adapting ideas from Jürgen Habermas (learning for emancipation), from Paulo Freire (raising consciousness leading to greater humanization), and from Latin American liberation theology (starting from experience and committed to transforming the world in the light of the Gospel), made the promotion of justice, peace, and freedom central aims within Catholic religious education, integrated within an approach that he calls shared Christian praxis. A warm, fluent, accessible, and inspiring communicator, Groome has attracted a wide following among academics and teachers at all levels in Catholic education, from primary/elementary through to university, although his approach has not been without critics.[27]

As the teachings of the Second Vatican Council became more embedded in church life, one of the fruits in Catholic universities was the major effort put into promoting service learning and education for social justice as integral to the mission of Catholic institutions.[28] A few examples can illustrate the links being made (in Catholic educational literature) between religious and spiritual priorities on the one hand, and a love that seeks justice for our neighbor in need on the other hand. First, a political scientist, reflecting on the relationship between a sacramental perspective and what goes on in institutions, reminds readers that "Representation of Christ occurs, not in mission statements, lectures, or exhortations, but in the daily work of nurses, aides, social workers, administrators, physicians, and pastoral staff."[29] Thus words about Christ must be enfleshed by living out what they imply; only then do they communicate effectively. Second, a commentator on Catholic schools in Canada argues that students in such schools should "scrutinize our politics, economics and culture through the lens of the beatitudes…. [There should be] a strong social justice component based on 'kingdom economics' integrated into every economics, business and technology course whose textbooks are most often based on 'the economics of the empire.'"[30] Thus Catholic education, far from being other-worldly, should be countercultural and prophetic. Third, with regard to students who have engaged in service learning, one observer maintains, "they have at times discovered life among the dying, happiness among the poor, joy and hope among the oppressed, and nobility among the suffering."[31] This type of educational experience seeks to overturn customary ways of thinking and valuing promoted by an acquisitive society. Fourth, another champion of Catholic education suggests that "social analysis goes beyond service and being kind. It requires individuals to study the causes of poverty, to work for more equitable and just treatment of people – especially the poor – and to risk their own status and standing for the sake of those less fortunate. Jesus was crucified because he spoke truth to power, and he calls those who wish to be Christians to do the same."[32] Such education is self-involving even as it reaches out to others; it challenges thinking even as it engages the heart. Spirituality calls upon the whole person; it entails a combination of passion, reason, and activity. As another commentator puts it: "If we act without passion and reason, we are robots. If we act without passion, we lack energy. If we act without reason, we become dangerous fools."[33] What all these writers have in common is their concern, as de Bary puts it, that "education must make a difference. It's not just an academic exercise."[34] And the only way it will make a difference to the lives of learners is if they realize that they can make a difference in the lives of others.

New emphases in political and liberation theology have prompted Catholic educators to adopt a preferential option for the poor, to attend more closely to the conditions for just teaching, to be aware of the close relation between coming to know right teaching and coming to do the right thing in one's life, and to be conscious of the need to model in classrooms and schools the kind of lifestyle to be pursued outside. Preparing for citizenship and being concerned for the common good are seen as integral, rather than irrelevant, to discipleship, even though there will always be tension (and sometimes contradiction) between the duties associated with the earthly kingdom and those that flow from fidelity to the Gospel. The spirituality/justice nexus is expressed in a number of related ways in Catholic education. Fresh understandings of the diverse factors that prevent full access to the goods offered in educational institutions have led to efforts by teachers toward greater inclusiveness. The experiences and perspectives of learners – and those of their families and communities – are taken more fully into account. If justice is one of the key virtues to be developed in students, then schools and colleges must exhibit justice in their operation, in student admissions, in staff selection and deployment, in designing curriculum, in assessing progress, in regulating community life, in celebrating worship, in the allocation of (human and material) resources, and in evaluating quality. One cannot teach justice (explicitly) if one fails to teach justly (implicitly). One cannot engage and develop the whole person in students without attending to their full personhood; this requires a discerning and open-hearted hospitality. The social and moral consequences of what is taught should be kept in mind. Special priority should be given to the needs of the disadvantaged and the stranger. Students should be encouraged to engage in acts of service that function simultaneously as occasions for learning. Collaborative learning is to be fostered, rather than merely individualist competition. Problems in the real world should be explored within the curriculum. Students should be helped to develop a sense of vocation, responsibility, and compassion.

Wolterstorff and Education for Shalom

Moving back across the Christian spectrum, Reformed Christianity has a strong history of investing in Christian schooling and of debating the proper aims and means of Christian education. The recently collected writings of Nicholas Wolterstorff, with whose comments regarding the separation of spirituality and justice we commenced these reflections, are referenced by several authors in this volume as well as expanded by his own essay. Those writings put forth a case for thinking of the aims and means of education in the light of the biblical vision of *shalom*. This Hebrew term, commonly – if thinly – translated as "peace," expresses a broad vision of human flourishing that refuses dichotomies between the spiritual and the social.[35] Wolterstorff's characterization of shalom reiterates many of the themes already mentioned:

> There can be no shalom without justice…. In shalom each person enjoys justice…. Shalom goes beyond justice, however. Shalom incorporates right relationships in general, whether or not those are required by justice: right relationships to God, to one's fellow human beings, to nature, and to oneself. The shalom community is not merely the *just* community but is the *responsible* community, in which God's laws for our multifaceted existence are obeyed. It is more even than that. We may all have acted justly and responsibly, and yet shalom may be missing: for the community may be lacking delight… shalom incorporates *delight* in one's relationships. To dwell in shalom is to find delight in living rightly before God, to find delight in living rightly in one's physical surroundings, to find delight in living rightly with one's fellow human beings, to find delight even in living rightly with oneself.[36]

Taking this vision of human flourishing as a starting point, Wolterstorff argues that Christian education needs to expand its horizons beyond a focus on academic excellence and personal piety to include education for compassion and for just action. This draws in pedagogical questions, such as how to call forth empathy and compassion on the part of students, how to confront them with the human faces of suffering, the role of modeling, and how to connect an emphasis on spiritual growth with the ability to lament. Here, once again, spirituality, justice, and pedagogy become intertwined.

The point of this brief catalogue of examples is not to suggest that the views of the educators cited are uniform, to endorse their particulars, or to imply that they are the only relevant examples, but rather simply to illustrate the fact that the essays in this volume are contributions to a continuing tradition of linking spirituality, justice, and pedagogy. That tradition may be in some ways countercultural in the present (or perhaps any) context, but it is nevertheless long and substantial. Each essay in the present volume tackles some particular aspect of the complex of issues raised by linking these matters – either by focusing on some particular area of teaching and learning, such as teaching engineering or history, or by questioning some particular part of the teaching and learning process, such as character formation or the role of spiritual disciplines in learning, or often both – and locates it against a backdrop of a faith-informed concern for the well-being of creation, both human and non-human.

The volume opens with the paper cited above, "Teaching Justly for Justice," in which Nicholas Wolterstorff argues for what he terms "primary justice" and its importance both as a main goal of teaching and a main characteristic of how we should teach. He says that Christian thinking about justice is too often limited to something that is meted out or the system that metes it out. But justice that is meted out presupposes the violation of primary justice (i.e., the justice that should characterize all our relationships at all times). It is this kind of justice that God loves and for which we should hunger and thirst. As a characteristic of relationships, justice focuses on the worth of the other. Teaching that is characterized by justice is therefore attentive to the worth of the other and to all the ways in which the other can be wronged, whether the other is the student or those about whom we learn in the classroom, whose writings we read, whose languages we study, or whose art we enjoy. Justice is not only a characteristic of good teaching, it is also a goal of teaching. We should aim at developing in our students a love of justice so that they think in terms of justice, are alert to the presence of injustice, and are disposed to pursue justice passionately.

Glenn Sanders's paper describes an attempt to do just that – to develop in his students a concern for justice through a course on the culture and politics of the modern Middle East. He was concerned not only to introduce the students to the Middle East region and to the Islamic faith of the majority of its people but also to provide opportunity for the students to reflect on why the issues met should matter to them and what it means to live justly. Making use of the work of Sharon Parks on spiritual development in young adults, Sanders aimed to develop what Parks terms a "mentoring environment" in which to develop "probing commitment." The course included provision for optional reflective journals on issues of justice in relation to the material being studied and group presentations to other students and to the wider college community that provided opportunity for the students to give expression to their developing commitments. Sanders's paper includes discussion of ways in which the course was successful and ways in which it failed to achieve its objectives. He concludes with evident faith in the value of the course and determination to improve upon it in future years.

The next paper in this collection also describes a pedagogical work in progress in the form of a case study of the Creation Care Study Program in Belize. The authors, Philip Fountain and Chris Elisara, see this program as an example of Wolterstorff's shalom model of education and they argue that "being there" through study abroad and field education may facilitate belief in an "earthy faith" that has space for an "earth justice" and an "earth spirituality." Fountain and Elisara see empathy as not only feeling for the wounded of the world but also as relationship "with places and people that are whole, delightful, and joyous." They contend that empathy can be encouraged pedagogically through field-based experiences "that enable students to see deeply, perceive interconnectedness, and comprehend creation in a sacramental light."

Doug Blomberg, in "The Formation of Character: Spirituality Seeking Justice," discusses what he sees to be major limitations in Howard Gardner's theory of multiple intelligences even though it has made a major contribution in setting forth "some of the rich complexity of being human." For all Gardner's talk of the intelligences as virtues, Blomberg argues that he focuses on "intellectual character" to the detriment of the moral and spiritual dimensions of humanness and human flourishing. Blomberg finds a needed reorientation in recent discussions of virtue ethics and goes on to advocate the integral perspective of a Christian holistic virtue ethic that is centrally concerned with restoring relationships and therefore with both spirituality and justice. Character is situated in "a creational, community context," and education should aim at the formation of character in such a context.

Steven VanderLeest turns our attention in his paper, "Teaching Justice by Emphasizing the Non-neutrality of Technology," to a particular relationship, that between justice and technology. He sets out to describe ways of teaching this relationship to students and of encouraging them to just action. VanderLeest argues that technological products are not neutral: they are designed, manufactured, distributed, and regulated so that their use has specific consequences. Technology is therefore biased and this bias can lead to injustice; norms of justice should therefore be applied to technological designs. VanderLeest goes on to list some case studies from the classroom that identify justice issues in what at first appear to be purely technical problems (e.g., reasons for the "digital divide," less energy-intensive lifestyles, alternative renewable energy resources, and the honesty of advertisements for computers). He also suggests some classroom activities and techniques to help in teaching of this kind.

In "Character Development from African-American Perspectives: Toward a Counternarrative Approach," Louis Gallien and LaTrelle Jackson call for character education programs for black urban youth in the USA that are culturally mediated and responsive in that they are "steeped in the history, literature, cultural, and religious values of African Americans throughout American history." This entails a "counternarrative approach" that is in sharp contrast to the majority culture European American meta-narrative in which character education is usually located. The rich resources of oral tradition need to be explored for stories "of courage and character endemic to the history of African-Americans," stories told and retold within the community, stories that facilitate the making of meaning by helping children and young people to say who they are and that promote a sense of direction by helping them to discover who they can become.

The final paper in this collection is Bradford Hadaway's "Preparing the Way for Justice: Strategic Dispositional Formation Through the Spiritual Disciplines." Hadaway argues that standard service learning courses encourage a student to practice just actions and may only be successful as transformational pedagogy if the student is already disposed to take justice seriously. Drawing upon certain aspects of Kant's view of the role of dispositional states, aspects that would bring Kant closer to advocates of virtue ethics, Hadaway distinguishes three kinds of disposition: "helping dispositions" that play a positive role in moral development; "uprooting dispositions" that undermine disruptive and destructive tendencies; and "bulwark dispositions" that counter and resist such problematic tendencies. He goes on to suggest that the spiritual disciplines of Trappist monasticism, especially as set forth by Thomas Merton, can provide models for a form of moral education that takes the student's whole dispositional set into account. For example, the spiritual discipline of simplicity can provide a bulwark against the negative disposition to take more than our share of available resources and thereby "prepare the way" for justice.

It is our hope that these essays will play their role in helping to "prepare the way" for justice and for spiritually responsive pedagogy in our classrooms, pointing us to fresh avenues of both thinking and doing.

Notes

1   Wolterstorff, Nicholas, "Teaching Justly for Justice," this volume.
2   Hill, Brian V., "'Spiritual Development' in the Education Reform Act: A Source of Acrimony, Apathy or Accord? *British Journal of Educational Studies*, 37:2 (1989) pp. 169-182.
3   Hay, David & Rebecca Nye, *The Spirit of the Child* (London: Fount, 1998).
4   Purpel, David E., & William M. McLaurin, *Reflections on the Moral & Spiritual Crisis in Education* (New York: Peter Lang, 2004).
5   See, e.g., Priestley, J., "Towards Finding the Hidden Curriculum: A Consideration of the Spiritual Dimension of Experience in Curriculum Planning" in *British Journal of Religious Education*, 7:3 (1985) pp. 112-119.

6   Keatinge, M. W., *The Great Didactic of John Amos Comenius*, 2nd ed. (New York: Russell & Russell, 1967) pp. 61-69.

7   Dobbie, A. M. O. *Comenius' Pampaedia or Universal Education*. (Dover: Buckland, 1986) p. 19.

8   Comenius, John Amos, *Panegersia, or Universal Awakening*, trans. A. M. O. Dobbie (Shipston-on-Stour: Peter I. Drinkwater, 1990) p. 70.

9   Comenius, John Amos, *The Orbis Pictus of John Amos Comenius*. (Syracuse, NY: C. W. Bardeen, 1887) p. 146.

10   Keatinge (1967) p. 66.

11   Dobbie (1986) p. 31.

12   Augustine, *The Literal Meaning of Genesis,* trans. J. H. Taylor, vol. 2 (New York: Newman Press, 1982) pp. 51-52.

13   Keatinge (1967) p. 72.

14   Keatinge (1967) p. 73.

15   Keatinge (1967) p. 214.

16   Dobbie (1986) p. 29.

17   Freire, Paulo, *Pedagogy of the Oppressed*, rev. ed. (New York: Continuum, 1996a).

18   Freire, Paulo, "Education, Liberation and the Church" in Astley, Jeff, Leslie J. Francis & Colin Crowder (eds.), *Theological Perspectives on Christian Formation: A Reader on Theology and Christian Education* (Leominster/Grand Rapids: Gracewing/Eerdmans, 1996b) p. 185.

19   Freire (1996b) p.170.

20   Freire (1996b) p.170.

21   Freire, Paulo, *Educação como Prática da Liberdade*. São Paulo, Brazil: Paz e Terra, 1999) p. 48, as translated by J. Elias in *Paulo Freire: Pedagogue of Liberation* (Malabar, FL: Krieger Publ. Co., 1994) and cited in Kristjansson, Carolyn, "The Word in the World: So to Speak (A Freirean Legacy)" in Smith, David I. & Terry A. Osborn (eds.), *Spirituality, Social Justice and Language Learning*. (Greenwich, CT: Information Age Publ., forthcoming 2007). This section is indebted to Kristjansson's more detailed account of Freire's spirituality.

22   Freire, Paulo, *Pedagogy of the Heart* (New York: Continuum, 1997).

23   For an authoritative summary of twenty-first century Catholic social teaching, see Pontifical Council for Justice and Peace, *Compendium of the Social Doctrine of the Church* (Rome: Libreria Editrice Vaticana, 2004); for overviews of the connection between salvation and liberation in Catholic thought, see Brackley, Dean, *Divine Revolution: Salvation & Liberation in Catholic Thought* (Eugene, OR: Wipf and Stock, 2004); and Martinez, Gaspar, *Confronting the Mystery of God* (New York: Continuum, 2001); for the potential of Catholic philosophy to contribute to public thinking on the common good, see Stiltner, Brian, *Religion and the Common Good:*

Catholic Contributions to Building Community in a Liberal Society (Lanham, MD: Rowman & Littlefield, 1999).

24   On the links between a changed understanding of the relation between the church and the world and a new concern for the common good in Catholic education, see Sullivan, John, *Catholic Education: Distinctive and Inclusive* (Dordrecht: Kluwer Academic Press, 2001) pp. 179-187.

25   See, for example, Krietenmeyer, Ronald, *Leaven for the Modern World: Catholic Social Teaching and Catholic Education* (Washington, DC: National Catholic Educational Assoc., 2000); Reidy, Pamela, *To Build a Civilization of Love: Catholic Education and Service Learning* (Washington, DC: National Catholic Educational Assoc., 2001).

26   Groome, Thomas, *Sharing Faith* (San Francisco, HarperCollins, 1991); Groome, Thomas, *Educating for Life*, (Allen, TX: Thomas More Press, 1998).

27   Questions have been asked about alleged defects in his ontology and epistemology, about whether he fails to do justice to the multiplicity of Christian interpretations of that faith, and about a tendency to conflate love of God *and* love of neighbor to love of God *by* love of neighbor (Martin, Robert, *The Incarnate Ground of Christian Faith*, [Lanham, MD: University Press of America, 1998]). He has also been accused (by Martin) of dissolving theology into anthropology, and soteriology into liberation, of inadequate treatment of the role of Christ in bringing together creatures and their creator, and by Murphy of conflating Christian education with a more universal (and abstract) understanding of religious education, and of excessive accommodation to the norms of liberal society, especially in confusing freedom with autonomy (Murphy, Debra Dean, *Teaching That Transforms* [Grand Rapids, MI: Brazos Press, 2004]).

28   See, for example, Reiser, William, *Love of Learning, Desire for Justice* (Univ. of Scranton Press, 1995); Toton, Suzanne, *Justice Education: From Service to Solidarity* (Milwaukee: Marquette Univ. Press, 2006).

29   Cochran, Clarke, "Institutions and Sacraments" in Sterk, Andrea (ed.), *Religion, Scholarship & Higher Education* (Notre Dame, IN: Univ. of Notre Dame Press, 2002).

30   Mulligan, James, *Catholic Education: Ensuring a Future* (Ottawa: Novalis, 2005) pp. 293-294.

31   Byrne, Patrick, "Paradigms of Justice and Love" in Wilcox, John & Irene King (eds.), *Enhancing Religious Identity: Best Practices from Catholic Campuses* (Washington, DC: Georgetown Univ. Press, 2000) p. 276.

32   Heft, James, "Truths and Half-Truths About Leadership" in Hunt, Thomas, Thomas Oldenski and Theodore Wallace (eds), *Catholic School Leadership* (London: Falmer, 2000) p. 212.

33   De Bary, Edward, *Theological Reflection* (Collegeville, MN: Liturgical Press, 2003) p. 111.

34 De Bary (2003) p. 164.
35 Wolterstorff, Nicholas, *Educating for Shalom: Essays on Christian Higher Education*. (Grand Rapids, MI: Eerdmans, 2004).
36 Wolterstorff (2004) p. 23.

Bibliography

Augustine, *The Literal Meaning of Genesis*, trans. J. H. Taylor, vol. 2 (New York: Newman Press, 1982).

Brackley, Dean, *Divine Revolution: Salvation & Liberation in Catholic Thought* (Eugene, OR: Wipf and Stock, 2004).

Byrne, Patrick, "Paradigms of Justice and Love" in Wilcox, John & Irene King (eds.), *Enhancing Religious Identity: Best Practices from Catholic Campuses* (Washington, DC: Georgetown Univ. Press, 2000).

Cochran, Clarke, "Institutions and Sacraments" in Sterk, Andrea (ed.), *Religion, Scholarship & Higher Education* (Notre Dame, IN: Univ. of Notre Dame Press, 2002).

Comenius, John Amos, *The Orbis Pictus of John Amos Comenius* (Syracuse, NY: C. W. Bardeen, 1887).

Comenius, John Amos, *Panegersia, or Universal Awakening*, trans. A. M. O. Dobbie, (Shipston-on-Stour: Peter I. Drinkwater, 1990).

De Bary, Edward, *Theological Reflection* (Collegeville, MN: Liturgical Press, 2003).

Dobbie, A. M. O. *Comenius' Pampaedia or Universal Education*. (Dover: Buckland, 1986).

Elias, J. (1994). *Paulo Freire: Pedagogue of Liberation*. Malabar, FL: Krieger Publ. Co., 1994).

Freire, Paulo, *Pedagogy of the Oppressed*, rev. ed. (New York: Continuum, 1996a).

Freire, Paulo, "Education, Liberation and the Church" in Astley, Jeff, Leslie J. Francis & Colin Crowder (eds.), *Theological Perspectives on Christian Formation: A Reader on Theology and Christian Education* (Leominster/Grand Rapids: Gracewing/Eerdmans, 1996b) pp. 169-186.

Freire, Paulo, *Pedagogy of the Heart* (New York: Continuum, 1997).

Freire, Paulo, *Educação como Prática da Liberdade*. São Paulo, Brazil: Paz e Terra, 1999).

Groome, Thomas, *Sharing Faith* (San Francisco, HarperCollins, 1991).

Groome, Thomas, *Educating for Life*, (Allen, TX: Thomas More Press, 1998).

Hay, David & Rebecca Nye, The Spirit of the Child (London: Fount, 1998).

Heft, James, "Truths and Half-Truths About Leadership" in Hunt, Thomas, Thomas Oldenski and Theodore Wallace (eds), *Catholic School Leadership* (London: Falmer, 2000).

Hill, Brian V., "'Spiritual Development' in the Education Reform Act: A Source of Acrimony, Apathy or Accord?" in *British Journal of Educational Studies*, 37:2 (1989) pp. 169-182.

Keatinge, M. W., *The Great Didactic of John Amos Comenius*, 2nd ed. (New York: Russell & Russell, 1967).

Krietenmeyer, Ronald, *Leaven for the Modern World: Catholic Social Teaching and Catholic Education* (Washington, DC: National Catholic Educational Assoc., 2000).

Kristjansson, Carolyn, "The Word in the World: So to Speak (A Freirean Legacy)" in Smith, David I. & Terry A. Osborn (eds.), *Spirituality, Social Justice and Language Learning.* (Greenwich, CT: Information Age Publ., forthcoming 2007).

Martin, Robert, *The Incarnate Ground of Christian Faith*, (Lanham, MD: University Press of America, 1998).

Martinez, Gaspar, *Confronting the Mystery of God* (New York: Continuum, 2001).

Mulligan, James, *Catholic Education: Ensuring a Future* (Ottawa: Novalis, 2005).

Murphy, Debra Dean, *Teaching That Transforms* (Grand Rapids, MI: Brazos Press, 2004).

Pontifical Council for Justice and Peace, *Compendium of the Social Doctrine of the Church* (Rome: Libreria Editrice Vaticana, 2004).

Priestley, J., "Towards Finding the Hidden Curriculum: A Consideration of the Spiritual Dimension of Experience in Curriculum Planning" in *British Journal of Religious Education*, 7:3 (1985) pp. 112-119.

Purpel, David E. & William M. McLaurin, *Reflections on the Moral & Spiritual Crisis in Education* (New York: Peter Lang, 2004).

Reidy, Pamela, *To Build a Civilization of Love: Catholic Education and Service Learning* (Washington, DC: National Catholic Educational Assoc., 2001).

Reiser, William, *Love of Learning, Desire for Justice* (Univ. of Scranton Press, 1995).

Smith, David I., "Biblical Imagery and Educational Imagination: Comenius and the Garden of Delight" in Jeffrey, David Lyle & C. Stephen Evans (eds.), *The Bible and the Academy* (Carlisle/Grand Rapids, MI: Paternoster Press/Zondervan, forthcoming 2007).

Smith, David I. & Terry A. Osborn (eds.), *Spirituality, Social Justice and Language Learning.* (Greenwich, CT: Information Age Publ., forthcoming 2007).

Stiltner, Brian, *Religion and the Common Good: Catholic Contributions to Building Community in a Liberal Society* (Lanham, MD: Rowman & Littlefield, 1999).

Sullivan, John, *Catholic Education: Distinctive and Inclusive* (Dordrecht: Kluwer Academic Press, 2001).

Toton, Suzanne, *Justice Education: From Service to Solidarity* (Milwaukee: Marquette Univ. Press, 2006).

Wolterstorff, Nicholas, *Educating for Shalom: Essays on Christian Higher Education* (Grand Rapids, MI: Eerdmans, 2004).

JE&CB 10:2 (2006) 23–37 1366-5456

Nicholas Wolterstorff

Teaching Justly for Justice

JUSTICE SHOULD BE both a hallmark and a main goal of teaching. Christian theology has tended to neglect the theme of justice and to limit its attention to retributive justice, rather than the more basic primary justice, that justice which has broken down when injustice occurs. Two reasons for this neglect are explored: the idea that love supplants justice in the New Testament, and the tendency for English translations of the New Testament to translate the Greek dikaiosunē *and related words in terms of rectitude rather than justice. The relationship of justice to personal worth is explored, together with reasons why teachers should focus both on teaching justly and on teaching for justice.*

My main theme will be that justice should be a hallmark of how we teach and one of the main goals of teaching; we should teach justly for justice. I intend the "we" that I have just used to cover all who teach. Everyone who teaches should teach justly. And justice should be one of the goals of any program of education – collegiate, secondary, elementary, whatever. The reasons I give for these conclusions will mainly be drawn, on this occasion, from Christian conviction; my principal addressees will thus be my fellow Christians. A good deal of what I say can be appropriated, however, by many of those who are not Christian; so I warmly invite them to listen in.

I

My impression is that most Americans today, when they hear of justice, think of *meting out justice*. They think of retributive justice. A good rule of thumb for listening to our politicians is that if the politician is talking about justice, assume that he or she is talking about prisons. Some Americans, when they hear about justice, think a bit more broadly than this; they think about the justice system in general. They think not only of meting out justice but also of what precedes that, namely rendering justice in cases of conflict and determining whether an accused is guilty of the accusation.

American Christians are no different from other Americans in this regard. When they hear of justice, they too tend to think of meting out justice or of rendering judgment. The tradition of Christian theology encourages them in this regard. The Christian scriptures speak over and over of God as just, of God as doing justice, of God as loving justice and hating injustice, of God as bringing justice, of God's justice. They speak of Jesus as the just one. But Christian theology abjectly fails to reflect this emphasis.

Aquinas, in his discussion of God in his massive *Summa theologiae*, takes God's justice and mercy together and devotes one very brief question to the pair (I.1.q. 21). In his earlier *Summa contra gentiles*, none of the 102 chapters devoted to a discussion of God and God's attributes deal with God's justice; God's justice gets mentioned only in a list of the moral virtues that God possesses (Chap. 93). In the *Systematic Theology* of the "scholastic" Dutch-American Reformed theologian, Louis Berkhof, there is a chapter devoted to the so-called communicable attributes of God, and in this chapter, a page and a third deals with what Berkhof calls the *righteousness* of God; under this rubric a few remarks are made about God's justice. In Karl Barth's vast *Church Dogmatics*, one part of one section of the volume devoted to the doctrine of God deals with the mercy and righteousness of God (the German, translated or mistranslated as "righteousness," is *Gerechtigkeit*).

Anselm, in his *Proslogion*, does somewhat better; he devotes an entire chapter to the topic of God's justice. His attention is focused entirely on God's retributive justice, however. He introduces his topic with the heading, "How the all-just and supremely just One spares the wicked and justly has mercy on the wicked." What he discusses is how God's mercy is compatible with God's retributive justice.

Obviously, this is only an extremely quick and shallow dip into the vast ocean of Christian theology. I submit, however, that it is representative: Christian theologians either say next to nothing about God's justice, or if they do discuss it with some care, what they have in mind is God's retributive justice. Whether the same pattern holds for what they say about human justice is, naturally, a different matter. Given the intimate connection in Scripture between God's justice and our justice, it would be surprising if it did not hold; but there is no necessity. In fact it does. For the most part, theologians do not speak much about human justice. And those who do speak about it at some length usually have in mind either *meting out justice* or *rendering judgment*. Justice, for them, is relevant to situations of conflict and to situations in which someone is accused of wronging someone. There are exceptions. Aquinas, for example, treats human justice at length and does not reduce it to meting out justice or rendering judgment.

The first thing I want to try to do is show how mistaken it is to equate justice with meting out justice or with rendering judgment. Meting out justice and rendering judgment deal with what justice requires when injustice has occurred or when someone charges that it has occurred. But if meting out justice and rendering judgment become relevant when injustice has occurred or is said to have occurred, then there has to be another kind of justice and injustice than that of meting out justice and rendering judgment. There has to be that kind of justice which has been violated or is said to have been violated. There has to be that kind of justice which has broken down or is said to have broken down. Call that kind of justice "primary justice." Only when primary justice has broken down or is said to have broken down do rendering judgment and meting out justice enter the picture.

What I am calling *primary* justice is often called *social* justice. My reason for calling it *primary* is not that I am against calling it social – not at all – but to highlight the fact that this kind of justice is basic. Unless there were this kind of justice, there could not be the kind of justice that most people think about most of the time, namely retributive justice.

My topic here is primary justice. Of course it is important to discuss what is to be done when primary justice breaks down – when somebody violates primary justice or is accused of violating it. But before we get to that, we have to have a clear view of what it is that has broken down – and of what things would be like if primary justice had not broken down. When the Scriptures say that God loves justice, part of what is sometimes meant is that God loves a well-functioning judicial system that deals justly with breakdowns in primary justice; but there can be no doubt that what God loves even more is the absence of breakdowns. God loves primary justice.

II

Why have so many Christians, theologians and laypeople alike, been so wary of employing the category of primary justice in thinking about God? And why have so many been so wary of employing the category of primary justice in thinking about human existence, in particular, Christian existence? Why has this been true in the past and why does it remain true today? Stanley Hauerwas, with social justice in mind, infamously remarked in one of his essays that "justice is a bad idea for Christians." I think he probably did not mean to say quite what that sentence means, taken literally and strictly. But a good many Christians would gladly affirm what it means taken literally and strictly. Social justice, they think, is a bad idea for Christians. Retributive justice is a good idea, but primary justice is a bad idea. Why do they think that, given that Scripture so emphatically tells us that God loves social justice?

No doubt a number of factors contribute to the eclipse of primary justice in Christian thought. Let me, on this occasion, confine myself to discussing two that seem to me especially important. The first is this: deep in the mentality of Christians is the conviction that in the New Testament, love supplants justice.

There can be no doubt that in the Christian scriptures, both the Old Testament and the New, there is a certain *superseding* of justice – note that I say superseding, not supplanting. Recall the psalmist's blessing of God:

> Bless the Lord, O my soul,
>> and all that is within me,
>> bless his holy name.
> Bless the Lord, O my soul,
>> and do not forget all his benefits –
> who forgives all your iniquity,
>> who heals all your diseases.
> The Lord is merciful and gracious,
>> slow to anger and abounding in steadfast love.
> He will not always accuse,
>> nor will he keep his anger forever.
> He does not deal with us according to our sins,
>> nor repay us according to our iniquities.
> (Psa 103:1-3, 8-10 NRSV)

God is blessed here for not dealing "with us according to our sins, nor repay[ing] us according to our iniquities." Out of mercy, grace, and love, God treats us in a way that goes beyond justice, that supersedes justice. Rather than repaying us according to our iniquities, God forgives us for our iniquities.

This theme of divine forgiveness that we find in the Old Testament is carried forward by Jesus in the gospels and refined by Paul in his letter to the Romans. God would have acted justly, says Paul, had he punished all human beings for their wrongdoing and infidelity. But out of grace, and on the basis of what Christ has done, God justifies all those who have faith. It is when it comes to the place of forgiveness in human life that the New Testament goes decisively beyond the Old Testament. Jesus teaches that as God forgives us for our wronging of God, so also we are to forgive those who wrong us. To this he adds the troubling converse: God forgives those who forgive.

Peter was disturbed by the open-endedness of Jesus' injunction to forgive. So one day he posed to Jesus the *reductio ad absurdum* question, "Lord, if another member of the church sins against me, how often should I forgive him? As many as seven times?" Jesus first gave a hyperbolic answer: not seven times but seventy times seven. Then he told the parable about the king who, out of mercy, forgave the large debt owed him by one of his servants, who, in turn, mercilessly refused to forgive the much smaller debt owed him by one of his fellow servants. The application of the story, in Jesus' words, is that you are to forgive your brother and sister out of mercy, from your heart, as often as proves necessary (Matt 18:21-35).

My point should be clear: in what they say about divine and human forgiveness, the Christian scriptures proclaim a certain superseding of justice. Forgiveness is not something that justice requires; the wrongdoer cannot claim a right to be forgiven. To forgive is to forgo one's right to retributive justice, and to do so not because the wrongdoer has a right to such forgoing but out of love or mercy. I suggest that it is especially the prominence of forgiveness in Christian scripture that has led Christians down through the ages to think that Christianity is about love, not about justice. Social justice may be a good idea for secularists of a progressive sort; it's a bad idea for Christians.

But let's take just a moment to look more closely at forgiveness. Yes, forgiveness is a certain superseding of justice. But note that one cannot dispense forgiveness indiscriminately hither and yon. I cannot forgive some Afghan farmer, whom I read about in the newspaper, for having violated the local law against growing poppies. I can forgive a person only if that person has *wronged me*, and only *for* the wrong he or she has done me. If you have not wronged me, then there is nothing I can forgive you for – though I may size up the situation incorrectly and *believe* that I can forgive you. I cannot forgive you for the wrong you did someone else, only they can forgive you for that – unless in some way your wronging of them was also a wronging of me. So now consider the wrong you did me for which I forgive you: that wronging of me for which I forgive you was a violation of primary justice. Forgiveness can only occur when there has been a violation of primary justice.

In short, though forgiveness does indeed supersede justice, the justice it supersedes is *retributive* justice. It cannot supersede primary justice; forgiveness presupposes primary justice – more specifically, it presupposes a violation of primary justice. The very action that is exemplary of God's actions and paradigmatic for ours, namely God's forgiveness, presupposes the reality of primary justice and of violations thereof. If there were no primary justice, and hence no infractions thereof, there could be no forgiveness. But divine forgiveness is at the core of the Christian gospel. To cut God's forgiveness out of the gospel would be to eviscerate the gospel. It follows that to cut primary justice out of the gospel, God's and ours, would be to eviscerate the gospel. God's love is not something other than justice; God's love presupposes justice. Rather than supplanting justice, it presupposes primary justice and injustice while superseding retributive justice.

III

Let me now move on to a second explanation of why so many Christians believe that justice is supplanted in the New Testament. This second explanation pertains to English-speakers. Suppose that you read the New Testament in the old Latin Vulgate or in a contemporary translation into one of the Latin-based languages, French or Spanish; the suggestion that justice has been supplanted in the New Testament will seem exceedingly strange to you. In the Latin Vulgate you will have found the word *justitia* all over the place; in contemporary French and Spanish translations you will have found *justice* or *justicia* all over the place.

Now take in hand a copy of the Latin Vulgate or a contemporary French or Spanish translation, and look for some occurrences of *justitia*, *justice*, *justicia*, or their grammatical variants. This won't be hard; there will be over 800 such occurrences. And now take in your other hand an English translation of the New Testament – it matters very little which one you take – and run some comparisons. Find an occurrence of *justitia*, *justice*, *justicia*, or a grammatical variant, and then look across at your English translation to see how it translates the passage. The probability is high that instead of the word "justice" or "just" you will find "righteousness" or "right."

The Greek being translated here is the noun *dikaiosunē*, the adjective *dikaios*, the verb *dikaioō*, and so forth. Latin and the Latin-based languages translate these *dik*-stem words with equivalents of our "justice" and "just"; our English translations for the most part translate them as "righteousness" and "righteous." In English we have "righteousness" and "righteous" coming from the Old German *recht*, and "justice" and "just" coming from the Latin *justitia*. Our translators strongly prefer the former to the latter in translating Greek words with the *dik*-stem.

Let me give you some examples. Since there are over 800 occurrences of *dik*-stem words in the Greek New Testament, my examples will constitute only a minute sample. "Blessed are those who hunger and thirst after *dikaiosunē*," says Jesus in one of the beatitudes as they are recorded in Matthew; our English translations read, "Blessed are those who hunger and thirst after righteousness." In a later beatitude Jesus says, "Blessed are those who are persecuted for the sake of *dikaio-sunē*"; our English translations read, "Blessed are those who are persecuted for the sake of righteousness."

If we arouse ourselves from the numbness of familiarity and actually think about this last saying, it begins to seem very odd. Righteous people are usually either ignored or admired; seldom are they persecuted. The people who pursue justice are the ones who get under people's skin and are persecuted. The first beatitude I quoted, as translated into English, strikes me as only a bit less odd. Maybe you can hunger and thirst after someone else's righteousness, though it strikes me as a strange thing to say; but it would be bizarre to say that you are hungering and thirsting after your own righteousness. It is justice that we hunger and thirst for.

You will notice that I am assuming that justice and righteousness are not the same. Justice is a normative social relationship. Maybe you can treat yourself justly or unjustly. But with the exception of that limiting case, justice and injustice require two or more people; justice and injustice pertain to how they are related. Righteousness, by contrast, is a character trait of individuals. In contemporary English the word has acquired the negative connotation of *self-righteousness*. Our English translators naturally hope that we will push that connotation out of mind. So the question is this: is Jesus, in these two beatitudes, talking about a normative social relationship or about a personal character trait? I think he is talking about a normative social relationship.

Let's take another example. Back a bit I said that the Christian scriptures speak of Jesus as *the just one*. Probably that will not have caught the attention of most readers. Those whose attention it did catch will probably have wondered where the New Testament speaks of Jesus as the just one. They don't recall ever coming across that. And indeed, they have not come across it if they have been reading the New Testament in English. But let's go back to the Greek. The centurion at Jesus' death "praised God and said, 'Certainly this man was *dikaios*'" (Luke 23:47). In one of Peter's speeches to a crowd in Jerusalem, after the death and resurrection of Jesus, Peter reproached his listeners for having rejected "the holy and *dikaios* one" and for asking instead "to have a murderer given to you" (Acts 3:14). And in the speech that Stephen gave at his martyrdom he accused his murderers of having killed "the *dikaios* one" (Acts 7:52).

In every English translation that is currently available for purchase you will find *dikaios* in all three cases translated as "righteous": Jesus is the righteous one. But once again, let us rouse ourselves from the numbness of familiarity and think about this. The gospel writers believed that what happened to Jesus in his trial and execution was a profound miscarriage of official justice. But what is relevant to a miscarriage of justice is not whether or not the person is righteous but whether or not he is innocent – innocent of the charge of having violated justice. Thus what Peter, Stephen, and the centurion were saying was that Jesus is the innocent one – in that sense, the just one.

It appears to me that there is among Christians a distinct unease with the idea that the one whom we worship was the victim of a miscarriage of justice; we feel more comfortable with the idea of Jesus as the sinless one. If we think of him as the sinless one, we elevate him above all humankind; if we think of him as the innocent victim of injustice, we make him all too human.

I must confine myself to just one more example. In Romans 1:17, Paul announces the main topic of his letter, namely "the *dikaiosunē* of God revealed through faith for faith." Every English translation currently available for purchase translates this as the *righteousness* of God revealed through faith for faith. Having announced the topic, Paul then proceeds to argue two main points. God's treatment of Gentiles is fully equitable with his treatment of Jews: God makes justification available to all who have faith, regardless of whether they are Jews or Gentiles. And this equitable treatment does not amount to God's breaking covenant with the Jews; God is not wronging Israel in offering justification to all. To my mind, what Paul is arguing here is not that God is upright but that God deals justly with God's human creatures, Jews and Gentiles alike.

You see the point. One of the reasons English-speakers think that justice has been superseded in the New Testament is that their English translations don't talk much about justice; they talk much more about love and righteousness than about justice. But these English translations are *mis*translations. I do not contend that all dik-stem words in the New Testament should be translated with grammatical variants on our word *justice*, none with grammatical variants on our word *uprightness*. It seems pretty clear that *dikaiosunē*, in the linguistic environment of the New Testament, could mean either *justice* or *rectitude*. The choice between these translations has to be made in terms of the thought of the passage in the New Testament in which the term occurs. My contention is that when one actually considers that thought, one sees over and over again that our English translations are mistranslations. The one whom we worship, Jesus Christ, was the *dikaios* one. He is both the one who inaugurates God's reign in which justice rules and the innocent one who was the victim of a miscarriage of justice.

IV

What is justice? I have to be extremely brief in my answer to this question. Everything that I say could be developed in great detail; everything that I say is in fact developed in great detail in the book I have just finished, which I call simply *Justice*. I think justice has to do with rights. Justice is present in social relationships when people are enjoying what they have a right to. The dark side of enjoying that to which one has a right is being wronged; to be wronged is to be deprived of that to which one has a right. Thus we could also say that justice is present in social relationships when no one is wronged.

In my view, a right is always a right to be treated a certain way by one's fellows – or in the limiting case, by oneself. That's why I said earlier that in distinction from righteousness, which is a personal character trait, justice is a normative social relationship. It is further my view that one's right to be treated a certain way by one's fellows is grounded in what respect for one's worth requires: if respect for my worth requires that I be treated in such-and-such a way by my fellows, then I have a right to such treatment.

Rights have been getting an even worse press from Christians in recent years than justice has been getting. Rights-talk, so it is said, reflects a self-centered, possessive, individualistic picture of society in which everybody is always talking about what he or she is entitled to rather than talking about what they ought to be doing and what the loving thing to do would be. I well remember a dear friend of mine getting up after a talk I had given about rights and, with quivering voice, saying, "Nick, nobody is entitled to anything; it's all grace!"

But that is mistaken. I acknowledge that rights-talk can be abused and often is abused; name me the kind of talk that is not abused. The battered wife is abused by the love-talk of those who say she should accept her abuse out of love for her husband; benevolence-talk was abused by the Afrikaners who talked of the benevolence they showered on the workers living in huts in their backyards. The other comes into my presence bearing claims on how to be treated, and I come into the other's presence bearing claims on how he or she treats me; for we are both creatures of worth. Rights-talk is for talking about those claims.

And let there be no doubt that we are creatures of worth. We have been made in the image of God. The psalmist can scarcely contain himself when he thinks about the exalted status that this gives us. Convinced that we human beings have been singled out from all other creatures for divine attentiveness and love, he asks in Psalm 8, "Who are we, that God is thus mindful of us?" The passage is rather often interpreted as if the psalmist's answer were, "We're nothing, we're worthless, just dirt and dust." But that is not the psalmist's answer. His answer is that we are created just a bit lower in the cosmic scale of worth than divine beings, or angels. The theme is picked up by Jesus at various points in the gospels when he speaks of human worth. "Consider the ravens," Luke reports him as saying (12:24 NRSV); "they neither sow nor reap, they have neither storehouse nor barn and yet God feeds them. Of how much more value are you than the birds!"

V

Christian teachers have long been urged to employ the categories of responsibility and love in thinking about what transpires in the classroom. I have joined in this; in 1980 I published a little book that I called *Educating for Responsible Action*. Without for a moment suggesting that the categories of responsibility and love are unimportant, on this occasion I want to stress the importance of employing the category of justice.

What does thinking in terms of justice do that thinking in terms of responsibility and love does not do? It places in the forefront of our attention the worth of the other. It alerts us to that worth and to what respect for that worth requires of us; and it alerts us to violations of that worth, to being wronged. What I have in mind by "worth" here is not just the worth we have qua human beings – the worth the psalmist and Jesus were speaking about – but also the particular worth that we each have: the worth of accomplishment, the worth of character, and so forth.

Responsibility does not focus on the worth of the other. Responsibility focuses on the agent, not on the object of our agency; it focuses on the rectitude or guilt of agents, not on whether the object of our agency has been wronged. When I as a teacher think of what transpires in the classroom in terms of responsibility, I attend to what I as agent ought to be doing and to what the students as agents ought to be doing. I attend to whether I did what I ought to have done; if I did, I judge myself as upright. And I attend to whether I did what I ought not to have done; if I did, I judge myself as guilty. Depending on how one thinks of responsibility, this can be an exceedingly impersonal way of thinking. All too often in the Christian tradition it has been impersonal – in particular, in the Calvinist tradition. Responsibility is thought of in terms of conformity to law. One's attention is focused on whether one's own actions and those of the students conform to law. That a person has been wronged falls out of view.

It is also true of love that it does not focus on the worth of the other – not, at least, if it is the justice-blind love that is regularly recommended by theologians as *agape*, rather than the justice-alert love of which

Scripture speaks. Justice-blind love, *agape*, thinks not in terms of the worth of the other but in terms of the well-being of the other. It seeks to enhance his or her well-being. And all too often it comes across as smothering; not infrequently, as oppressive. If I only think in terms of enhancing your well-being, not at all in terms of what respect for your worth requires, then I will see myself as justified in imposing all sorts of hard treatment on you, just provided that I think it has the potential of greatly enhancing your well-being. I will torture you if I think that torture is likely to save you from hellfire. One can understand why Hannah Arendt remarked that the problem with Christians in politics is that they love too much.

Do not misunderstand me. I am not saying that the categories of responsibility and of love are irrelevant to the classroom. What I am saying is that in the absence of the category of justice, they are all too likely to produce deeply distorted and oppressive ways of thinking and acting. Attentiveness to justice and injustice means attentiveness to the worth of the other and to all the ways in which the other can be wronged.

What makes such attentiveness especially important for teachers is the discrepancy of authority and power in the classroom. Teachers stand before the students as authority figures with power at their disposal; that makes it very easy for them to wrong the students. I am well aware of the fact that there are some teachers, especially at the college and university level, who dislike this discrepancy of authority and power and try to eliminate it by introducing discovery-learning strategies, by purporting to function as nothing more than discussion leaders, and the like. My own view is that these always amount to ways of concealing authority and power rather than eliminating it; and that if the teacher really does do nothing more than lead discussions, it's likely that the students are being wronged.

I may have given the impression, with these remarks about teaching justly, that teaching justly pertains only to the relation between teacher and students. If so, let me correct that impression. In one way or another, a wide range of human beings turns up in the engagement of teacher with their students. We read their writings, we read the writings of others about them, we study their languages, we are enriched by their art. All of them are to be treated with due respect for such worth as they have; none is to be treated abusively. Abusive speech is rampant on the American scene today; civil discourse is on the ropes. It pains me to acknowledge that certain groups of Christians are second to none in the abusive way they treat and speak of their fellow human beings. It should not be. One of the hallmarks of Christian education should be that no one speaks abusively. Whatever criticisms we may lodge against our fellow human beings are always to be set within the context of the recognition that these other human beings are like us in that they too are created in the image of God and redemptively loved by God. They have a right to be treated with respect. Justice requires that one treat them thus.

There is a second way in which teaching justly is not confined to how the teacher engages students. There may be something unjust about the composition of the class. It may reflect unjust discrimination, whether on the part of the teacher or on the part of others. If that is the case, then no matter how justly the teacher treats the students he or she actually has, the teaching is not, and cannot be, fully just. Injustice inheres in these being the students the teacher is teaching, rather than certain others.

VI

I opened my discussion by saying that justice should be both a hallmark of how we teach and one of the main goals of teaching; justice should be both the adverbial modifier and the object of the verb *to teach*. We should teach justly for justice. I have discussed justice as the adverb; let me now say something about justice as the object.

What do I mean when I say that we should teach for justice, that justice should be one of the main goals of what we teach for? Not the only goal, mind you; but one of the main goals. I mean that we should aim at cultivating in students an alertness to the presence of injustice and a disposition to pursue justice; we should aim at cultivating in them a love of justice. For in loving justice, they are like unto God. Recall the testimony of the psalmist and the prophets: "I the Lord love justice" (Isa 61:8; Psa 37:28). And recall the ringing declaration of the prophet Micah, known to all of us:

> He has told you, O mortal, what is good;
>   and what does the Lord require of you
> but to do justice, and to love kindness,
>   and to walk humbly with your God. (Mic 6:8 NRSV)

How do we do this? How do we teach for justice? For one thing, we teach for justice by teaching justly. That is to say, we teach for justice by modeling justice; we teach for justice by making the classroom itself a place of justice. I judge that I do not have to belabor this point for those who read this essay; I do not have to defend my assumption that one of the most effective ways of cultivating in people the disposition to act a certain way is oneself to act that way – to model that way of acting.

Instead of defending that assumption, let me highlight another assumption that I am making here and that I have been making throughout. I noted that most Americans, including most American Christians, when they hear talk about justice, think about meting out justice and about rendering judgment; retributive justice is prominent in their minds. That's not true for everybody, however; some do think about primary justice, about social justice.

My experience with these latter has been that the primary justice they usually have in mind is the great big issues of social justice: human rights and the violations of human rights. In my comments about our worth qua human beings I have indicated my belief in the importance of human rights. But I have come to think that it is a mistake to begin one's reflections about justice and about teaching for justice with human rights. Rights, along with the honoring or violating of rights, pervade the fine texture of our existence; they pervade the fine texture of the classroom. If I fail to give a student the grade he deserves because I just don't like him – he's too nerdy, too pushy, too wheedling, too arrogant, whatever – I have treated him unjustly, deprived him of what he had a right to. I well remember a landlady that my wife and I once had who was intensely alert to the injustice being perpetrated on the Hungarians by the Russians but stupefyingly insensitive to the injustice that she herself was perpetrating on some of her renters. That was cheap liberalism. Or was it cheap conservatism? I don't know. What I do know is that it was cheap. All her attention was focused on gross violations of human rights to the ignoring of the fine texture of injustice in which she herself was enmeshed and that she herself was perpetrating.

Modeling is important. But to be truly effective in cultivating dispositions, modeling needs the support of articulated thought. If teaching justly is to be effective as a model, it needs the support of a conceptual framework for thinking about justice. Students have to be taught how to think in terms of justice – which means thinking in terms of worth, of respect for worth, of violations of worth, of wronging the other, and so forth. It is here especially that the scholars of the Christian community have a contribution to make: the biblical scholars, the theologians, the philosophers, the social ethicists, the social theorists.

A few weeks ago, a member of my church who teaches in one of the Grand Rapids colleges asked what I was doing in my retirement. I told him that I was working hard on a book on justice – working "like a mad dog" is what I actually said. He must have made some bland response; I don't remember what it was. But the next week he came up to me and said that he had been taken aback by my saying that I was working on a book on justice. He himself never really thought in terms of justice, nor did the people he associated with; love was what was important for him. But he would be open to learning from what I came up with.

Half of this reaction was typical, half, atypical. The typical half was his comment that he and those he associated with never thought in terms of justice – I presume he meant primary justice. As I indicated earlier, I think that is typical not only of present-day American Christians but of the Christian tradition generally. The atypical half of his reaction was his comment that he would be open to learning from what I came up with. The more typical reaction would have been starting an argument with me, or not bothering but just walking away with the thought that here is one more of those secular liberals who are infecting the church.

The Christian story is the story of the inauguration by Jesus of God's just rule; of Jesus' falling victim to a gross miscarriage of justice; and of God's merciful justification, on the basis of what Jesus did and underwent, of all who have faith. To cut justice out of the Christian gospel is to cut out its heart. Until our scholars undo the eclipse of primary justice in Christian thought, we cannot effectively teach for justice. Of course we don't just have to sit around waiting for our scholars; we can prod them, make them feel uncomfortable.

Allow me to make one last point concerning teaching for justice. A central component of teaching for justice is cultivating in students an alertness to injustice and a corresponding passion for seeking justice. It is my experience that most people are not like the landlady of whom I spoke. Her passion for justice to the Hungarians was evoked, so far as I could tell, entirely by newspaper accounts of the Russian invasion of Hungary. Most people are not like that, or not very much like that. Newsprint does not evoke in them a passion for undoing injustice. Much more effective is fiction. And more effective yet is seeing the faces and hearing the voices of victims, whether in person or on film or TV. My own experience has been that the plight of the Palestinians did not much bother me until I actually met some of them and heard their stories. I very much doubt that I am peculiar in this regard. Justice for the handicapped will not touch the hearts of most of us until we see and hear them and listen to their stories; justice for people of color will not touch the hearts of most of those of us who are without color until we see and hear them and listen to their stories. The passion for justice is empathy's child.

VII

Those who are into spirituality are usually not into justice, and those who are into justice are usually not into spirituality. The burden of my discussion has been that spirituality and justice must be joined. A spirituality that is faithful to the Christian scriptures is a spirituality that incorporates justice. A love for justice that is faithful to the Christian scriptures is a love that echoes God's love for justice and walks in the footsteps of Jesus Christ, the just one.

JE&CB 10:2 (2006) 39–62   1366-5456

Glenn E. Sanders

Exposing Students to Intractable Problems: Christian Faith and Justice in a Course on the Middle East

THIS CHAPTER DESCRIBES the planning and teaching of a course on the history of the Middle East at a Christian university, focusing in particular on the way in which a concern for spiritual growth and for engagement with issues of justice shaped the structure and pedagogy of the course. The chapter explores the "inner" and "outer" work necessary to connect justice concerns with spirituality and learning.

The announcement for a well-conceived academic conference will lead the previously "unengaged" to rethink assumptions and approaches to topics, disciplines, and tasks. Such was the effect of the Calvin College conference "Spirituality, Justice, and Pedagogy" on my history and political science course "Middle East: Culture and Politics," last taught during fall 2005. Common sense, numerous sermons, and my reading of Nicholas Wolterstorff and Parker Palmer suggest that these three concerns fit together. Yet how do they fit, exactly – especially if the cultivation of young adult sensibilities is primary? How might a course bring together personal spiritual growth and a concern for political and social justice? How might it do so concretely, with intense attention to real-life situations and responses?

A course on the culture and politics of the modern Middle East can encourage students to rethink notions of justice in relation to their personal faith experiences by confronting them with long-standing, complex realities of political and religious difference. The conceptualization necessary for a concrete course forced me to reconsider presuppositions about teaching, justice, and spirituality, in particular about the best ways to build a fruitful synergy between the student's growth, the teacher's presence, and the community's need. Course planning required the exploration of different types of assignments than had been used in previous versions of the course. Most significantly, first implementation –

even if halting and in ways unsuccessful – proved the viability of bringing personal spiritual growth and a concern for political and social justice together through a set of assignments structured in line with Sharon Parks's theories of student spiritual formation and informed by specifically Christian spiritual content. I hope that my personal narrative will help other teachers as they design courses with similar goals.

Conceptualization

At first glance the benefits of using a course on the Middle East to address issues of spirituality and justice seem self-evident. What better topic to confront students with concrete, complex issues of justice? What better subject matter to lead Christian young adults to think through preconceptions about the relationship of religion to justice; about the historical, political, economic, and cultural forces that prolong injustice; about practical responses available at the local level? With its focus on Islamic tradition, regional modernization, genocide, national identities, terrorism, etc., the course on the Middle East seemed a good testing ground.[1] The environment was hospitable: a class of about thirty, mostly Christian believers, at a small denominational college in the southern plains.

My presumptions about the ease of the project nonetheless soon confronted three realities: first, the difficulty of formulating applicable definitions and concepts of justice – let alone Christian concepts of justice – appropriate for undergraduate students; second, the problem of designing a course that adequately matched student cognitive development, assignments, and the justice emphasis; and third, the pesky thought that even with clear definitions and a good course design, the attempt to evaluate historical incidents and current policies and events in light of justice concerns will always be difficult and even questionable, given the problems of applying moral categories while avoiding "Whig history" or self-interested judgments.

Then there was a fourth problem that, although related, stood apart from the other three. It is much easier to *talk* about relations of spirituality and justice than to *build* them. Conference literature asked hard questions about the relationships between spirituality and learning and between spirituality and teaching. It was this aspect of the conference that was initially most intriguing; it was this aspect that seemed hardest to address, given the existential vagaries of the "spiritual life" and its operation within particular "spiritual communities." For example, what exactly can a particular Christian tradition and experience (American and Protestant) contribute to a student's understanding of the region and to his or her sympathies toward those who suffer injustice?

Initial responses to the first two problems depended on specialists. For definitions and concepts of justice I first looked to three colleagues who delivered guest lectures in the opening days of the course on concepts of justice in the Old Testament, the New Testament, and recent philosophy. These lectures were to serve as summaries of current ideas and a basis for later class discussions. They emphasized the centrality of justice in the Judaic tradition, the tight bond between justice and Jesus's teachings about God's kingdom, and the different modern philosophical approaches to social justice (utilitarianism, libertarianism, the ideas of John Rawls, etc.).[2]

The second problem – concerning cognitive development and course design – led to reflection on Sharon Parks's descriptions of student development in mentoring environments. *Big Questions, Worthy Dreams* builds on the research of Carol Gilligan, William Perry, James Fowler, and other developmental theorists. It provides a useful description of the "developmental spiral" from the "adolescent/conventional" to the "young adult" to the "tested adult" and finally to the "mature adult." Parks emphasizes that teachers can promote cognitive and spiritual growth among young adults by working within categories of "imagination," "moment," and "mentoring." It seemed clear that specific topics and assignments might intentionally facilitate the processes that she describes. Her model also provides some important ways to address the fourth issue, concerning the relations between spirituality, learning, and teaching.[3]

The third problem – on the appropriateness of using justice concepts to evaluate events, trends, and ideas – proved difficult to solve in the abstract, but at least moderately approachable in the concrete. Simply to admit the possibility of the problem is to make some headway. Consciousness of the potential for biased misreadings of history or current events is a first step toward limiting their influence. In addition, internationally accepted standards of justice, such as the UN Declaration of Human Rights and more recent developments in international law, can provide some indication of current consensus. Non-governmental organizations such as Amnesty International and different Christian denominations also provide standards that *de facto* link ideals about justice – even if inchoate – to specific events and trends.

The broader moral and intellectual contexts are also important when gauging the appropriateness of including concerns about justice. Historians have always weighed different explanations, maintaining an interpretative balance between historicism and the need for a "useful" history that relates in some way to current experiences. The modernist ideal of value-free interpretation has proven chimerical. All interpretation proceeds from particular values; the best one can hope for is a temporary, intentional suspension of judgment followed by tentative conclusions based on best evidence. This suspension of judgment flows from the compulsion and moral responsibility to pursue truth rather than to avoid it as impossible, nonexistent, or uncomfortable.

This compulsion to tackle the problem boils down to the main reason for risking intellectual and pedagogical integrity: that the Christian calling to witness about God's redemptive kingdom in Christ should lead to honest and deep explorations of all human experiences, with only provisional answers possible in this life. The primary goal of my teaching has increasingly become to seek an authentic Christian perspective, then to infuse it into the study of particular, complex realities – historical, political, social, and cultural – and to do so with as much intellectual integrity, imagination, theological learning, and grace as possible.

This goal suggests my concern over the fourth problem, the conference's "spirituality" emphasis, and my conviction that serious teaching and learning should have at their center the influence of things spiritual – Christian faith in particular. I have begun to look for specifically Christian theological statements on justice that would clarify the task for me. One of the best so far has come from James McClendon's *Ethics*:

> The resurrection is the acted word in which God identified his own immortal life, once and for all, with the life, the life story, of Jesus of Nazareth. In this event-that-is-God's Word, this enacted word, this historic sign, Christians "hear" the vindication of the story of Jesus, of his way. In this event, Jesus' way is designated henceforth to constitute God's own way for his people. Thus the resurrection is the reestablishment of the community of the Israel of God (Gal. 6:16) on a new basis, vindicating the justice of God in the older establishment, and promising that very justice, through Christ, to all the world.[4]

Dietrich Bonhoeffer's *The Cost of Discipleship*, John Howard Yoder's *The Politics of Jesus*, and other works provide definition and inspiration as I continue to reflect on the character of justice and the calling to do it.[5] With regard to the complexities of the Middle East, the course needed not only to introduce students to the region and to Islam but also to include spaces for reflection on questions like "Why concern oneself so deeply with such political, social, and cultural issues?" and "What would it mean for one to live justly in relation to this region, especially as one better understands the origins and character of suffering there?"

Parks's analysis of post-adolescent spiritual development provided a basic framework for posing these questions to students. She emphasizes the need for teachers to create "mentoring environments" in which "emergent adults" feel comfortable probing the commitments of adolescence. Such environments allow the asking of "big questions" while at the same time fostering a sense of belonging, even toward those one senses as "different." A mentoring environment also encourages students to cultivate "habits of mind" that take the developmental process forward (her list includes dialogue, critical thought, connective-systemic-holistic thought, and contemplative mind). Finally, such an environment communicates images (of truth, transformation, etc.) and "communities of practice" that will draw the emergent adult toward a sense of moral purpose.

This environment can only have such effects if a young person also works within his or her own "fragile inner-dependence." The emergent adult struggles toward a more resilient and confident inner dependence that may someday itself become a realization of the interdependence of all things. This process occurs through various operations of the imagination, which Parks describes as occurring in five "moments," essentially the common stages of self-reflection: conscious conflict, pause, insight, repatterning, and testimony. According to Parks, the end result would not necessarily be a definitive answer, but "tested commitment" and even "convictional commitment" to an answer that has arisen authentically from within the student and remains respectful of other perspectives, acknowledging the interrelationships between complex moral responses.[6]

Growing in particular from James Fowler's work on the stages of faith,[7] Parks's analysis at least suggested a dynamic to encourage within and among my students and some categories for assignments. It helped concerning the relationship between general spirituality and learning by suggesting a theoretic description of distinct psychological and spiritual responses within a particular environment. Her analysis did not do so from a particular historical or theological position, however, nor did it clearly address the tie between spirituality and teaching. My compulsion for a practical engagement of personal faith and world complexities demanded an overtly (although not necessarily exclusively) Christian perspective. My responsibility as professor also made me an intimate partner in the game.

These two concerns led to two deeper problems, existential in character. I am a partner in the game, a mentor; thus the question arises, How should I "be with" my students? The spirituality of my presence – whatever that might be – would exercise itself naturally at a superficial level. For the mentoring relationship to develop and have strong influence, however, my own spiritual practice – the spiritual disciplines, for example – would become a concern. The second problem stemmed from the necessary particularity of the Christian spiritual heritage: What could I *do* in the course to take advantage of this tradition, while both maintaining fundamental academic and intellectual integrity and respecting (for example) Muslim views on justice? The classroom is not a prayer or revival meeting. The students are at different places in their spiritual journeys. At the same time, the goal of engaging complex realities from an authentic faith remains fundamental.

Considerations such as these operated more or less subliminally as course goals and methods took shape. I found it useful to think about interrelated classroom processes in terms of student, teacher, and specific external communities, because spiritual growth occurs in multiple communities at multiple times. "External community" here can be any group outside the classroom: the student body of a college, a church congregation, city hall, etc. It may be intimate (e.g., a family) or abstract (e.g., a government). In any case, from one moment to another, student, teacher, and (any given) community interrelate through perceptions, goals, shared ideals, etc.

Each of the three has "inside" and "outside" work to do. The division is mainly for convenient description, with definitions of "inside" and "outside differing some from the conventional. Both are forms of self-reflection. Inside work is initial self-reflection on receptivity toward other people and ideas. Outside work starts from reflection on receptivity but then moves toward appropriate response and action, all the time critically measuring motive, effect, next response, etc. The following table suggests a nexus for spiritual development in the classroom:

	Some goals for the student	Some goals for the teacher	Some goals for specific external communities
Inside work	The probing mind, the receptive heart	Mentorship through listening – best ways to listen, best ways to respond (questions, images, etc.)	Exposure to the needs and inner realities of others; the problematizing of individual and collective motives; an appreciation of significant fundamentals
Outside work	Intense reflection on appropriate individual spiritual responses to deep knowledge of conditions; individual planned and unplanned actions	The modeling of spiritual practice, responses; provision of images and tools for student spiritual responses	The education and mobilization of public opinion, to create public solidarity; the cultivation of "best practices" over a lengthy period

Parks suggests the difference between the two forms of student work when she emphasizes that the emergent adult works from within a fragile inner dependence that finally requires the "wing-stretching" of "testimony."[8] Both inner work and outer work are interrelated parts of spiritual growth, but each has its own focus, either on motivation, appreciation, and receptivity, or on embodiment, encouragement, and relationship.

The inside work for the teacher and community is different from the student's. The teacher's work is "mentor self-formation," although this fact points to the clear fact that such inside work always involves relationships. These categories are not air-tight. That community exists as part of the process suggests that a community is not an inert "context" with aspiritual "objects" as its members, but that a community exists to influence both student and teacher, and that the classroom – where student and teacher work together – can influence the collective spiritual experience of the external group. For example, this reference to community inside work suggests the traditional role of Judeo-Christian "prophecy" in public reform. One thinks of Elijah training Elisha, and the kings of Israel having to cope with both of them.[9]

So if the grid identifies the work that should go on in this dynamic of spiritual growth, what is the next step? Parks calls for the mentoring environment to encourage so-called moments that emphasize conflict, otherness, and critical reflection.[10] A course on the modern Middle East provides a natural and fruitful medium for these emphases, with its substantial, interrelated problems:

- First, ethnic, religious, and cultural *difference*, best represented to college-aged Christian believers as the "Muslim Other."
- Second, historical, social, and economic *complexity*, best seen in issues such as the Arab-Israeli conflict, the Iranian Revolution, U.S. regional involvement, etc.
- Third, the *intractability* of twenty-first-century political and social realities, best represented by Palestinian-Israeli relations, systemic inequalities of wealth, etc.
- Fourth, issues pertaining to *modernity*, including regional democratization, the rise of Islamist terrorism, etc.

These four problems of difference, complexity, intractability, and modernity together provide "space" and impetus for the kind of self-reflection that can bring spiritual growth. A particular dialectic quality to each allows for even more opportunities:

- *Commonality* qualifies difference, as American Christians encounter Middle Eastern Christians or realize the common cultural experiences of Muslims and Christians from the region.

- In some instances complexity gives way to *simplicity*, especially when injustices are clear (e.g., genocide).
- The *possibility of solution* sometimes qualifies a seemingly unremitting intractability (e.g., the end of the 1975-90 Lebanese civil war).
- The problem of modernity must address the veneration of *tradition* and the inertia of past practice, for good (e.g., the social benefits of Islam) or ill (e.g., autocratic political practices).

To summarize so far: the course should thus deal with the four problems of difference, complexity, intractability, and modernity (and their dialectic variations) regularly within Parks's typology of student development and through the dynamic represented by the grid of "inside" and "outside work" for student, teacher, and communities. The focus on justice translates into specific questions: just to use the most prominent example, "What does a consideration of *justice in general* bring to the problem of complex Palestinian-Israeli relations? What does a *specifically Christian ideal of justice* bring?" Because Christian love in this case requires close listening to other perspectives, this work should delay a response until the opportunity, for example, to compare and contrast such Christian ideals to Muslim ideals of justice.

And finally, the type of question most important for spiritual development arises: "How do I as a Christian believer understand the place of justice in, for example, the Palestinian-Israeli conflict, and what can I as a believer do to promote justice in this case?" It bears emphasis that the grid represents the contribution of a spiritual dynamic to a course that otherwise might address cognitive and moral development but would not take seriously the listening skills, the positive motivations, the important virtues such as perseverance, self-control, peace-making, and love that are to flow from a spiritual life. At this junction it becomes important to include the spiritual disciplines as aids, and also to reflect deeply on fundamental questions of a spiritual or theological nature. The Christian tradition brings a particular set of responses based on the primacy of justice as a form of love, the blindness of fallen humanity to the character and extent of suffering, the possibility of redemption through Christ's sacrifice and the Holy Spirit's presence, etc. Teacher and students should do their particular work through a cultivation of Christian spiritual disciplines. For example, if I am to grow as a teacher/mentor, I need to reflect prayerfully and conscientiously upon the virtue of hospitality and listening, then practice it in the context of the course. Similarly, as my students confront the differences between Christianity and Islam, serious thought about Christ versus the Qur'an as the Word of God needs to include not only a cognitive understanding of the differences but a serious, personal exploration of the spiritual implications that flow from these fundamentally different starting places. It also needs to go slowly in concluding what to do. A rush to judgment based on insufficient reflection could lead to a lack of respect toward Muslims, even an aggressive "spiritual imperialism," also a blindness to practical responses that might on the surface seem unspiritual or un-Christian. Finally, this situation suggests that the influence of specifically Christian spiritual insights will remain limited and problematic. It is one thing for a teacher and students to cultivate the spiritual disciplines; it is quite another for external groups to benefit similarly, given the character of modern pluralism. Such influence is an entirely different matter that requires further exploration elsewhere.

Planning

How did these reflections translate into concrete assignments and classroom emphases?[11] First, some way to gauge my students' actual understanding of Islam and the Middle East seemed appropriate. A pretest included questions of fact ("When did Muhammad live?"), understanding ("What does jihad mean? Explain briefly."), evaluation ("The primary force behind the establishment of the State of Israel was...."), and opinion ("Should the U.S. have gone to war in Iraq?"). The pretest also included a broad, open-ended question on the definition of justice. This short quiz thus situated the course material directly within a consideration of justice.

Second, throughout the semester students were to submit eight short papers. Two were responses to readings and class discussions on justice ("How would you define justice?") and Islam ("How has your reading about Islam conflicted with your preconceptions about the religion?"). Two more – on traditional and contemporary Islamic culture – were responses to documentary or art films.[12] A discussion of a chief theme in Nagib Maghfouz's Palace Walk was the fifth paper. Finally, students summarized what they had learned from three recent documentaries.[13]

Third, the primary locus for spiritual reflection was an optional "justice journal."[14] Students could replace one or two 75-point exams with a journal that included one or two substantial reflections a week on the relationship of justice concerns to recently studied material. For example, discussions about Islam's origins and character could lead to reflection on the nature of justice in Islam and the Qur'an's many counsels to social justice. From that consideration a student might explore the similarities and differences of Islamic ideals in relation to the Jewish, Christian, and philosophical perspectives treated in the guest lectures.

Fourth, to address community needs, pairs of students began in mid-semester to research a particular "hard problem," with some attention given to identifying justice issues, evaluating according to justice ideals, etc. Then the class was to divide in half, with one member from each pair in one of the two halves. Each pair-member was to teach his or her part of the class about the pair's hard problem. Classmates would then offer feedback, and the pairs would reassemble and prepare a public presentation on the problem. Late in the semester, the class would put up display boards, video presentations, etc., in the student center. The goal of such public presentations would be to teach the college community (including trustees and administrators) about the Middle East, pertinent justice issues, and possible Christian responses to real-life complexities in another part of the world.

It may prove impossible for the broad college community to address issues of justice from a collective spiritual perspective. Simple seed-planting is a poor substitute for serious interaction, however. The optimum situation would be for the presentations to address directly and graphically the "principalities and powers," modern versions of "the structured world of power and authority that [stands] over against the kingdom of Christ."[15] The extended analyses of these forces by McClendon and others suggest the complexities and ambiguities of confronting them, also the difficulty of formulating meaningful and coherent Christian responses. And the subtleties necessary in a serious report might easily get lost on the student body and even faculty and administration. The goal is nonetheless worthy, especially if students take matters beyond the public presentations and talk with friends and acquaintances about key issues. Follow-up discussions with student honors societies might yield fruit. A recent issue of *Christian Scholar's Review* focused on Islam, and a gathering of faculty members to discuss cogent articles at the same time that public presentations were on display allowed good conversations with colleagues about Christian-Muslim relations, comparative approaches to parallel biblical and Qur'anic texts, and the use of Islamic novels at a Christian college.[16]

For the students the presentations should act as Parks's "testimony" does in the process of spiritual and cognitive growth. It is a service-learning project of sorts. Students determine their own topics. The goal is for presentations to which students feel compelled to commit. A presentation should be more than interesting; it should have import for personal spiritual growth. For that purpose I asked that each presentation try to consider the issue of justice. The goal was for serious presentations not on Arabic music but on Palestinian protest music, not on *jihad* but on Islamist notions on the justice of terrorism, not on urban planning but on the equity of housing distribution in Cairo.

First Implementation

I have taught "Middle East: Culture and Politics" eight times, each time differently. Given that fact, I should have anticipated the integration of a justice emphasis to be difficult. It both was and was not. Within the first month of class, I fell into the common trap of treating the course as a regular upper-level history offering, ignoring student difficulties with foreign names, concepts, and events. Perhaps in a subconscious attempt to compensate, I increasingly ignored the daily assigned readings, getting behind in the process. Some students became frustrated, stopped reading, and became increasingly disengaged in the coursework. Completion of assignments got delayed. The eight short papers proved too many, despite my requiring only limited research. Needless to say, class morale dropped. To concern oneself and students with matters of spiritual growth and justice in such a situation was challenging, to say the least.

I had planned during the semester to use regular online evaluations to keep track of morale, general understanding, etc., but I put their use off, only arranging to get feedback from all the students finally at the end of the semester by having the class meet in a computer lab. I plan to schedule regular feedback sessions in the lab during the next time that I teach the course. If I had scheduled the regular evaluations this time, I could have addressed some of the fundamental problems during the semester. In any case, these problems should prove easy to address; I have already started course revisions (such as streamlining assignments and reorganizing lectures).

The root issue was that I tried to do too much. Despite having cut material used when teaching the course before, new material on Islamic terrorism, the Arab-Israeli conflict, and the like, made up the difference, and I never managed adequately to return to issues of justice during class time.

But despite this "tacked-on" quality of the justice emphasis, even my flawed efforts yielded fruit, some far beyond my expectations.

First, the simple inclusion of the emphasis made a difference for some students. Many had never thought much about justice as a topic, let alone as a responsibility for Christian believers or as a category for the exploration of an academic subject. They had not considered the classroom a site for spiritual growth. Even after only the first unit (on justice) and the definition paper, however, one student wrote on an evaluation, "The paper was tough for me – and I'm far from satisfied in the definition upon which I settled – but because of it this thing of justice has been on my mind constantly." Another wrote, "Before I solely thought that justice was the correct 'revenge' that takes place but now I see that justice when God-inspired can provide a fairer and more peaceful world when we as a large community all work toward achieving justice." The ability of some students to read Jesus's command in the Golden Rule as a call to justice suggests Parks's notion of probing commitment among emergent adults and an openness and respect toward personal spirituality's contribution to living the just life.

Second, while some students let the course's problems get in the way of engaging the material, such was not the case for many, especially with regard to the contemporary culture and documentary writing assignments, for which the students were to watch recent films and documentaries and to submit brief reports. Some of the films posed hard questions easily connected to issues of justice. "Osama" concerns the plight of a twelve-year-old girl and her family in Taliban-ruled Afghanistan. In order to survive, the family has the girl pose as a boy. Forced to attend a *madrasa*, the girl is recognized and forced to marry an elderly Taliban leader. Students regularly struggled with the fundamental unfairness of the girl's plight, the treatment of women under the Taliban, and the systemic religious, political, and economic problems underlying the story. "Control Room" required a disclaimer because of some strong language, but several students wrote on the documentary's pointed analysis of press freedom during wartime. The film compares and contrasts al-Jazeera coverage of the 2003 invasion of Iraq with U.S. press coverage.

In a related vein, many students enjoyed Mahfouz's *Palace Walk*.[17] A realistic treatment of an Egyptian family ca. 1919 à la Hugo, the novel contains significant representations of both traditional roles for women and nationalist responses to British colonialism. The novel is too long, but a shorter one should elicit similar responses. Similarly, the public presentations did fulfill their original goal more or less. The level of student engagement and the quality of presentation differed noticeably, but some student projects, such as those on the UN Relief and Works Agency, women's rights, and the nature of *jihad* reflected fruitfully on issues of justice and communicated these reflections to the college community successfully.

Finally, for those students who took their journal writing seriously, the justice journal did indeed address the issues and categories of spiritual growth that Parks had suggested. Below are two especially revealing excerpts related to Christian faith and the modern nation-state:

Student 1:

> I had a friend who joined the Marines. He was a very thoughtful, emotionally deep and godly man. Throughout his training he told us little about what went on, yet he did mention a few

instances where the men were treated as dogs. After finishing his training he was completely unable to relate to others on any sort of emotional level, especially those who brought out the deepest emotion, including his mom. Relationships, edifying ones, were severed because he had been taught to rely solely on himself and the corp.

Where does justice come into play in this scenario? Those left broken and confused from this abrupt severing of relationship – where does their relational responsibility lie? Where is his? The corps? It is difficult to understand this mindset in an objective manner. On one hand it seems completely absurd to brainwash and beat men into submission, to the point that families struggle to survive, where relationships are destroyed. Yet on the other, these men are being trained to stay alive. So is this technique justified in the fact that it teaches them to live in a war-zone setting?

All of this leads me to another question. What does this teach us about life? We are taught in church that God has created us to be beings of relationship with Him and with each other. And I have learned this semester that the responsibilities to maintain these relationships are a part of justice and righteousness. Yet at times life seems to be nothing beyond simple survival. At these times it is common for one to shut down and become guarded in their relations with others. But where is this line between our need for relationship and our need for survival? They seem to need each other, yet are so contrasting at times that they seem to eliminate one another.

I suppose justice comes when one gives one's heart to God, who heals and protects it. Then when moments of pure survival come upon us and our earthly relationships fail, we have our relationship with God to fall back on, tying the two together. Now it is the upholding of relationship that allows us to survive.

Student 2:

A lot of my friends want to laugh at me because I sound like a disciple of Daniel Quinn, but I borrow many of his ideas and theories in my dislike of the concept of the modern nation-state. I think that it defies nature, the environment, the natural organization of humankind into tribes. It supports population explosion, large-scale industry and production (which in the modern world is entirely antithetical to this biosystem), and its very roots are in the assumption that humankind rules the world.

These sorts of issues have been on my mind throughout the lecture topics on the beginnings of nationalism in the Middle East. I wonder this: how just – to the environment, to tribes, to humankind's natural inclination for wandering – is it to own land? To decide on borders and boundaries for a certain group of people in a certain part of the world and to cut others off from crossing them?

Is it natural? Would any supreme deity appreciate this sort of manipulation of its creation? The nation instills a sense of pride in its inhabitants – but isn't pride "wrong" or "immoral," at least within the Christian tradition? It creates the concept of the other, of "us and them," protagonist and antagonist. And is that ever correct?

Why have we divided the world as such? Why are we content to let it remain this way? I feel sometimes that God must be crying over our destruction. Destruction isn't just. Justice does not extend only to humankind, though we tend to think that way. We are unjust to the earth.

A third student took to using short quotations as a spur. She always found these herself. Here she reflects on one from the Christian tradition; elsewhere she uses the Qur'an, Abraham Lincoln, and others.

"You [God] have not only commanded continence, that is, from what things we are to restrain our love, but also justice, that is, on what we are to bestow our love." – St. Augustine

I have never thought of justice itself as being a form of love. I have thought of it as love towards the "victim" but never of it being love in itself. But I guess that justice is right action towards all things, and that right action should always be love. Love is right action and right action is justice. Can wrong action be just? Sometimes. I think that your loyalties are tried, and you can't seem to love either side or do justice to either. Can a lack of justice be just? No, I don't think it can, but I know that humans certainly have the capacity to be unjust, if not just at all.

The most painful realization that I carry away from the course is the rich opportunity missed by my not providing adequate opportunity for collective examination of such intense reflections, either in class or in small groups.

Nonetheless, the benefits of a focus on justice in a course on the modern Middle East are clear. The emphasis allows deep thinking and deep feeling to work side by side. It allows a specifically Christian witness to influence understanding and response while encouraging comparison and contrast of that witness with other traditions and perspectives (e.g., Islamic; modern humanist). It potentially engages big, meaningful themes from within local experience (e.g., individual encounters with Muslims; nationalism).

And while I will struggle to find the best ways to patiently and thoughtfully apply the spiritual virtues (inner work) to assess and treat real-world conditions sensitively and reflectively (outer work), with Christian love rather than Christian triumphalism, and while I will similarly struggle to find and communicate appropriate and fruitful models of justice in specific situations, I nonetheless feel the course is headed toward what Arthur Holmes has described as "doxological learning." One of his four primary emphases in the renewal of an overtly "Christian academy," doxological learning involves "reflecting on how whatever we do in life relates to its creator and lord. It makes life and learning a continuous doxology of praise to God."[18] The character of "praise" in this case relates to a sense of humility in confronting difference, complexity, the intractability of problems, and transitions to modernity. Praise also involves the intellectual exercise of assessing historical, political, social, economic, and cultural forces with the need for justice – God's kingdom – in mind. Finally, praise includes the inner journey of learning how to "bless" the particular situation – by explaining it well and truthfully, by motivating oneself and others to sympathy and respect, and by suggesting redemptive actions, both individual and collective.

Notes

1   Given the historical and contemporary significance of Islam for both politics and culture in the Middle East, the course presently gives only passing attention to the place of Judaism and Christianity in the region. My students often know little about Islam, and the trade-off with this emphasis seems appropriate. In addition, despite an expectation that Christian young adults might assume the dispensational eschatologies of popular novels or particular preachers, such has very seldom been the case, at least among the conventional students who attend my institution. On the contrary, they tend toward the opposite extreme – a hard-nosed appreciation of power politics tempered by an insistence for secular humanitarianism (cf. Smith, Christian & Melinda Denton, *Soul Searching: The Religious and Spiritual Lives of American Teenagers* [New York: Oxford

Univ. Press, 2005]). Given both media influences and ignorance of the region, students often "over-islamicize" the Middle East, forgetting the importance of Palestinian Christians, for example, or failing to appreciate significant differences between Muslims.

2   See appendix one.

3   Parks, Sharon, *Big Questions, Worthy Dreams: Mentoring Young Adults in Their Search for Meaning, Purpose, and Faith* (San Francisco: Jossey-Bass, 2000) pp. 34-157. See below for further details on Parks's model.

4   McClendon, James William, *Ethics: Systematic Theology* (Nashville: Abingdon, 1986) p. 249.

5   Bonhoeffer, Dietrich, *The Cost of Discipleship*, trans. R. H. Fuller (New York: Touchstone, 1995); Yoder, John Howard, *The Politics of Jesus: Vicit Agnus Noster* (Grand Rapids, MI: Eerdmans, 1994).

6   Parks (2000) pp. 53-157.

7   Fowler, James, *Stages of Faith: The Psychology of Human Development and the Quest for Meaning* (New York: HarperCollins, 1981).

8   "Testimony. We do not seem to fully grasp the new insight, and we are not entirely at ease with it, until we express it in our own terms. What was once inchoate now wants to be given form. We are drawn into an act of creation" (Parks [2000] p. 121).

9   Cf. 1 Kings 19:19-2 Kings 13:20.

10 Parks (2000) pp. 104-126.

11 See below "Appendix Two: Course Syllabus."

12 These included a locally-produced video on Islamic Spain, PBS's "Islam: Empire of Faith," and the commercially available films "Osama," Baran," "The Color of Paradise," and "Secret Ballot."

13 Students selected from "Control Room," "Jenin Jenin," and PBS *Frontline*'s "Muslims," "Al Qaeda's New Front," "House of Saud," and "Israel's Next War?"

14 I realized the benefits of the journal only after I had required the exams. Also, *mandatory* self-reflection on justice concerns did not seem an appropriate way to promote spiritual growth. About a dozen students took the option. Impression suggests that they did so to take advantage of the justice emphasis, to hedge their final grade, to avoid the pressure of an exam, to customize their schedules with relation to other classes and assignments, or a combination of these motives and others.

15 McClendon (1986) p. 161.

16 *Christian Scholar's Review*, 34:4 (Spring 2005). Essays include Ida Glaser and Gregory M. Anderson, "Building Respect, Seeking Truth: Towards a Model for Muslim-Christian Studies" (411-424); Yohanna Katanacho, "Christ is the Owner of Haaretz" (425-441); David H. Vila, "Arab Christians and Islam: Conflicts and Contributions" (443-461); Henry Luttikhuizen,

"The Place of the Sacred: Islamic and Christian Visual Cultures in Medieval Spain" (463-485); Michael Lodahl, "Disputing over Abraham Disputing with God: An Exercise in Intertextual Reasoning" (487-504); David W. Landrum, "Teaching Islamic Novels in a Christian College" (505-518); and David Holt, "Notes on Acts 10 from the Middle East Studies Program" (519-530).

17   Mahfouz, Naguib, *Palace Walk*, trans. William Maynard Hutchins and Olive E. Kenny (New York: Anchor Books, 1991).

18   Holmes, Arthur F., *Building the Christian Academy* (Grand Rapids, MI: Eerdmans, 2001), 5.

Bibliography

Bonhoeffer, Dietrich, *The Cost of Discipleship*, trans. R. H. Fuller (New York: Touchstone, 1995).

Christian Scholar's Review, 34:4 (Spring 2005) pp. 407-530.

Fowler, James, *Stages of Faith: The Psychology of Human Development and the Quest for Meaning* (New York: HarperCollins, 1981).

Holmes, Arthur F., *Building the Christian Academy* (Grand Rapids, MI: Eerdmans, 2001).

Mahfouz, Naguib, *Palace Walk*, trans. William Maynard Hutchins and Olive E. Kenny (New York: Anchor Books, 1991).

McClendon, James William, *Ethics: Systematic Theology* (Nashville: Abingdon, 1986).

Parks, Sharon, *Big Questions, Worthy Dreams: Mentoring Young Adults in Their Search for Meaning, Purpose, and Faith* (San Francisco: Jossey-Bass, 2000).

Smith, Christian & Melinda Denton, *Soul Searching: The Religious and Spiritual Lives of American Teenagers* (New York: Oxford Univ. Press, 2005).

Yoder, John Howard, *The Politics of Jesus: Vicit Agnus Noster* (Grand Rapids, MI: Eerdmans, 1994).

Appendix One: Guest Lectures on Justice

Professor Kevin Hall, "Justice in the Hebrew Bible"

JUSTICE AND RIGHTEOUSNESS: This prominent biblical hendiadys (see Amos 5:21-24) suggests that justice is fundamentally and broadly concerned with fulfilling the demands of relationship. Thus, Tamar is more righteous than her father-in-law Judah and pursues justice (see Genesis 38:1-26).

JUSTICE AS RESPONSIBILITY: Whereas many notions of justice tend to the issue of rights, justice in the Hebrew Bible conceives of justice in terms of mutual responsibilities. Related biblical concepts that manifest this conception of justice include covenant and *hesed*, a Hebrew term blending the idea of love and loyalty. (See Micah 6:6-8: "Do justice, love *hesed*…")

INJUSTICE AS EXPLOITATION: Oppressive relationships of domination and abuse display most clearly and disturbingly lack of justice. Cf. Israel's deliverance from oppression (Exodus 2:23-25) and the warnings contained in the Covenant Code (Exodus 22:21-27).

THE PURSUIT OF JUSTICE: The divine commitment to justice – especially as rescue of those oppressed (see references under #3) – leads to the ubiquitous biblical call to pursue justice through active resistance to oppression (see, again, Amos 5:21-24).

JUSTICE AND SPIRITUAL DISCIPLINE: Because injustice is rooted in the greed so ingrained in the human condition, the pursuit of justice remains a constant challenge requiring commitments and disciplines that provide the renewal necessary to sustain the pursuit. Thus, Sabbath-keeping is linked in the Hebrew Bible to the pursuit of justice and community (see Isaiah 58 and Amos 8:4-6; also, cf. the two reasons given for Sabbath-keeping in Exodus 20:8-11 and Deuteronomy 5:12-15).

Professor Bobby Kelly, "Justice in the New Testament"

JESUS AND THE GOSPELS: MARKS OF THE KINGDOM: For Jesus, everything revolves around the kingdom, the central theme of his ministry. Jesus announces that God is becoming king, the rule of God is beginning. The injustices that exist are soon to be eradicated. Luke's gospel emphasizes the theme of justice, so pivotal to the whole concept of the kingdom of God.

- Care for the Poor: Mary's song (Luke 2:46); the programmatic words of John the Baptist (3:7ff), and of Jesus (4:16ff); Jesus condemns the Pharisees for their love of money (16:14); Zaccheus' entrance into the kingdom is confirmed by sharing of wealth with poor (19:8); Sermon on the Plain is focused on blessings to the poor and woes to the wealthy (6:20-26).

- Confrontation of Oppressive Authorities: Much of Jesus' conflict is with the priestly aristocracy, which works closely with the Roman authorities. The operation of the temple is in the hands of the power brokers. The two recent chief priests, Annas and Caiaphas, enjoyed unrivaled power as a result of collaboration with Rome. Note the focus of the Baptist's call for repentance is upon tax collectors and soldiers (Luke 3:10-14); the parable of an unjust judge (18:1-8); and Jesus' response to the question of taxation (20:20-26).

- Abolishment of Violence: Jesus has harsh words for Herod, who seeks to kill him (Luke 13:31-33); the centurion's remark using the word for "just" (23:47); the condemnation of those who carry out acts of violence against the kingdom (compare Luke 16:16 and Matt. 11:12).

- Acceptance of All People: Samaritans (Luke 9:51-55; 10:33; 17:16); tax collectors and sinners (15:2 and his radical table fellowship); a tax collector is the hero of the parable (18:9-14) and conversion of Zaccheus (19:1-10); Luke mentions eleven women otherwise unknown in the gospels. Shepherds and women bookend the two great events of history, indicating the gospel is for all people.

ACTS: A continuation of the emphasis in Luke's gospel with the overall purpose to justify the Gentile mission. Note also the important summary statements highlighting a community of justice (2:43-47; 4:32-35).

PAULINE LETTERS: Paul is the apostle to the Gentiles. While Paul might not have the volume of writings advocating justice, he certainly leads the way in producing one people, with distinctions between Jew and Gentile obliterated. Paul extends this principle of equality beyond ethnicity and includes gender and status (Gal. 3:28). Finally, Paul shows concern for the poor in the collection for the church at Jerusalem that seems a critical part of his work among the Gentile churches (Rom. 15:25-29; 1 Cor. 16:1-4; 2 Cor. 8-9).

GENERAL EPISTLES: JEWISH CHRISTIAN COMMUNITY: James makes the strongest statement for justice: for the widows and orphans (1:26-27) and the hungry and needy (2:14-17) as evidence of genuine faith, for equal treatment of rich and poor (2:1-7); and harsh condemnation for the acquisition of wealth at the expense of the poor (5:1-6).

REVELATION: Apocalyptic is the literature of people in their experience of powerlessness and oppression. As a genre it asks why God allows the innocent to suffer and why the wicked are allowed to rule. Its purpose is to provide hope for a persecuted minority community. Finally it affirms God's justice will not allow the oppression to continue forever.

Professor Randy Ridenour, "Concepts of Justice in Contemporary Philosophy"

"For every complex problem, there is a solution that is simple, neat, and wrong."
– H. L. Mencken

UTILITARIANISM

- Components: consequentialism, impartiality, and maximization

- Objections
  - Free Rider Problem
  - Incompatible with justice
  - Cannot accommodate moral rights

RAWLS

- Principle of Greatest Equal Liberty: Each person has an equal right to the most extensive liberty compatible with a similar liberty for everyone else
- Principle of Fair Equality of Opportunity: Offices and positions should be genuinely open to all under conditions of fair equality of opportunity
- Difference Principle: Social inequalities should be arranged so that they are of the greatest benefit to the least advantaged
- Original Position: no one is aware of how their circumstances will be in civil society
- Objections
  - Hypothetical contract cannot ground moral obligation
  - The contract would not necessarily result in the Difference Principle

LIBERTARIANISM (NOZICK)

- Non-consequential: respect for the inviolability of moral rights
- Redistribution is typically unjust
- Minimalist state: secures peace, enforces contracts, protects against aggressor states, etc.
- Objections
  - No adequate foundation for libertarian rights
  - Can be inconsistent

EGALITARIANISM

- Ideal is equality, but equality of what? 1) Resources 2) Welfare
- Walzer: Justice is created by each community. Each distinct social good has its own sphere of justice with its own criterion of distribution. Equality requires that no one be able to dominate over others.
- Objection: Results in a cultural relativism in which there can be no objectively wrong distributions

ASSOCIATIVISM: Relational facts are morally significant, because we identify with associates

JUSTICE AS MUTUAL ADVANTAGE: Justice is the set of rules that it is rational to follow for mutual advantage

Appendix Two: Course Syllabus (Extract)

Course Requirements: HIST/PSC/SASW 301A, Middle East: Politics and Culture

CATALOG DESCRIPTION: "A survey of Middle Eastern history from Muhammad to the present, with special attention to politics and culture. The course focuses on the development of Islam and its political, social, cultural, and intellectual effects; the rise and decline of the caliphate; the rise and decline of 'gunpowder' states during the early modern period; the origins of modern Middle Eastern nationalism; and the development of current political and cultural conflicts in the region. The course is preparatory to the model League of Arab States held each spring. Prerequisite: US 116."

GENERAL DEPARTMENTAL GOALS: The Department of History and Political Science has adopted these five general goals as important for OBU students of History:

1. **Knowledge and appreciation of specific facts:** History graduates should demonstrate a knowledge and appreciation of specific facts from U.S., European, and non-Western history (including a general knowledge of geography) and some appreciation of the significance of those facts, both within historical contexts and today.

2. **Narrations and analyses:** In clear prose and oral presentation, history graduates should be able to narrate and analyze an event or evolution, including the delineation of cause and effect.

3. **Secondary arguments and primary sources:** In clear prose and oral presentation, history graduates should be able to analyze and evaluate an argument in a secondary work and to demonstrate the significance of primary materials, in part by considering serious problems raised by the argument and sources.

4. **Research:** History graduates should be able to collect research on a topic and synthesize that research to present an extended narrative and/or analysis and/or argument in clear prose and oral presentation.

5. **Historiography and theory:** History graduates should demonstrate general knowledge of major issues in U.S., European, and non-Western historiography and specific knowledge of chief theoretical problems.

PRIMARY COURSE GOAL: To evaluate Middle Eastern history, politics, and culture in light of recent ideas on the nature and goals of *justice* – in particular, identifiably Christian ideas on justice.

SECONDARY COURSE GOALS: This course focuses on the *description* ("what?"), *explanation* ("why?"), *analysis* ("how?"), and *evaluation* ("why significant?") of important events, trends, and individuals in the Middle East, ca. 600 to the present, through an intense collective exploration of primary sources.

Five sets of questions suggest the chief themes/subjects for the semester:

1. What is *Islam*? How has Islam evolved from its origin to the present? What are the primary features of *Islamic civilization* (learning, art, literature, architecture, etc.)? How have these been influenced by modernity?

2. How did Middle Easterners respond to *political, economic, and cultural modernity during the nineteenth century*, in particular the rise of nation-states and a global economic system?

3. What forces influenced the *evolution of the Middle East during the twentieth century*? In particular, what effects did decolonization, the discovery of oil, the establishment of Israel, the growth of secular nationalism, and the rise of Islamism have?

4. What is contemporary *Islamism*? What are its relations to recent acts of *terror*? Is there truly a "clash of civilizations" (Huntington) going on?

5. What are *current American policies toward major Middle Eastern states*? In particular, how has American support for democratic movements shown itself (or not) in Afghanistan, Egypt, Iran, Iraq, Israel, Jordan, Kuwait, Libya, Pakistan, the Palestinians, Saudi Arabia, Syria, and Turkey? Have other American interests proven more important than support for democracy?

REACHING THESE GOALS: This course will try to fulfill both general and course-specific, primary and secondary goals through the following assignments:

	Abilities	Assignments
Description	("what" questions: "characters," "story," chronology) ↓	Daily reading, map test ↓
Explanation **Analysis**	("how" questions: cause and effect relations) and ("how and why" questions: understanding of context) ↓	Papers, presentations, exams
Evaluation	("so what" questions: argument, synthesis, judgment)	Papers, presentations, exams

CLASS ASSIGNMENTS:

- **Daily reading:** Each day I will ask whether you have completed the day's readings. I'll also ask you about what you didn't understand in your reading. Your accumulated positive responses and your attention to the reading in daily discussions will determine your score.
- **Map test:** A test early in the semester will encourage you to learn the key geographical features of the Middle East.
- **Short papers:** Most of your points this course will come from eight two-page responses. Some will require limited research. See separate instructions.
- **Pair presentation:** Pairs of students will work up a presentation on a controversial subject, then each will make the presentation to half the class and receive feedback.
- **Public presentation:** Using the pair presentation and feedback as a starting place, each pair will prepare a related public presentation suitable for performance or display in the student center. At the end of the semester the class will teach the OBU community about major current issues in the Middle East.
- **Essay exams:** There will be three essay exams. See below for dates. Exams have short answer identification questions plus essays. The final is comprehensive.

Maximum scores possible:

Daily assignment	=	50
Map test	=	50
Short papers (50 points each):	=	400

- Justice definition paper
- Islam paper
- Traditional culture review
- Contemporary culture review
- Mahfouz review
- Documentary reviews (3)

Pair presentation	=	50
Public presentation	=	100
Essay exams:		

- Islam = 75
- Midterm = 75
- Final = 200

Total	=	**1000**

Grade by total points scored:

1000-900	=	A
899-800	=	B
799-700	=	C
699-600	=	D
Below 599	=	F

Grading criteria: You will be graded on:

- Your thoroughness in preparing your reading
- Your contribution to the collective work (class discussions, presentations, etc.)
- Your ability to compile ideas and materials and present these in a clear and concise manner
- Your ability to explicate documents and use them to describe, explain, analyze, and evaluate an event or trend (i.e., to demonstrate how evidence supports an interpretation, to trace cause-and-effect, to identify important questions for further study, etc.)
- Your ability to identify and address the chief problems – past and present – for interpreting the character and significance of Middle Eastern politics and culture
- Your ability to do library and Internet research and draw solid conclusions from your research

JE&CB 10:2 (2006) 63–90   1366-5456

Philip Fountain and Chris Elisara

Being Is Believing? Out-of-the-Box (Subversive) Education[1]

THE WOUNDS OF this world – ecological and humanitarian – require a re-thinking of our educational systems. Building upon a shalom model of education, the authors argue that questions of space and location are critically important to Christian pedagogies. Our education praxis must move beyond the classroom to engage students empathetically in the world around us. Doing so will necessarily be a subversive endeavor. The Creation Care Study Program in Belize is presented as a case study of "study abroad" and field-intensive education.

Being and Believing

What is the value of "being there"? How is "being there" educationally useful? Are we, in our normal education practice, simply not "being there" enough? Is being (there) believing?

As an inquiry into "being there," this paper presents a case study of how space, place, and location bear upon what Wolterstorff has termed a "shalom" model of education.[2] In particular, this paper explores the educational praxis of the Creation Care Study Program (CCSP) as it pursues a shalom-based educational mission that seeks to inspire students toward an "earthy faith," a Christian faith engaged with and responsive to the world that is our home, in Belize, Central America.[3] As a study-abroad program grounded in field-intensive courses, CCSP provides an example of an alternative Christian education that relocates the critical but often forgotten element of "being there" at the center of its pedagogy. We argue that direct experience facilitates a rich learning space in which empathic bonds – critical for inspiring understanding, action, and engagement – can flourish. Being there can help inspire belief. However, we also know that being there is not believing. Utilizing alternative spatialities can help educators elicit responses from students, but student responses cannot be controlled or directed in such spaces any more than in the traditional classroom. Space or location is a critical variable in education; however, it is not the only variable, nor is belief ever that simple.

This paper was written by reflexive practitioners, both involved in the leadership of CCSP, and represents our reflections on our craft: tertiary education of the study-abroad variety. The descriptions and analysis we provide are therefore the result of our having been there, assisting in the education of the students who attended the program. Initially, the paper was an intentional attempt to stand back and think critically about the value of our task and method. For CCSP this process was exceptionally valuable. The paper is offered here in the hope that it may inspire and help other Christian educators to reflect on their own craft, especially in the light of the wounds of this world and the healing that Christ offers.

CCSP is part of a substantial and growing movement of Christian organizations and individuals that are seeking to provide a meaningful response to key issues facing our world. This movement intentionally seeks to reflect the whole gospel of Christ. Particularly, our perspective is informed by a prophetic strand of evangelicalism, one that sees all people and societies as in need of transformation. The message of Christ, as presented in the Scriptures, presents a radical call for change to all. Christ's gospel finds us – our societies, cultures, religions, educational theories and practices – wanting and calls us to an alternative world, to different priorities, to new things. This sense of the prophetic nature of Christian faith undergirds our work in education.

On Believing In Shalom

At the center of CCSP's educational philosophy is the biblical concept of shalom. Our mission statement reads: "CCSP is a Christian organization whose mission is to educate students to be a part of, and agents for, God's shalom, particularly through understanding and caring for creation." We are heavily indebted here to Nicholas Wolterstorff's writings on education and justice, which we have found helpful and challenging. We believe they display a vision adequate to the task and calling of Christian education.[4]

What does it mean to participate in the kingdom of God? What is the biblical vision of the Christian-in-the-world? Wolterstorff responds by asserting the centrality of the biblical concept of shalom, the existential reality of the reign of God. The purpose of the Christian church is to pray and struggle for shalom, celebrating its presence and mourning its absence.[5] Shalom is therefore also the goal of Christian education; it is to exhibit and equip for shalom.[6] But what is shalom? According to Wolterstorff, the Scriptures describe shalom as God's desire for a broken and hurting world. It encompasses the whole breadth of our relationships, including those "with God, with self, with fellows, with nature."[7] This is no disembodied "evangelical gnosticism."[8] This is embodied individuals and communities in relationship with the earth in which they have been placed, and with the Author of the universe.[9] Flourishing is at the heart of the vision of shalom: the God of life desires life in its fullest. There are three key parts to Wolterstorff's understanding of shalom.

- Shalom involves the *absence of conflict and violence*. Shalom is a total commitment to seeking peace, both with and for humanity and with and for the rest of creation.
- Shalom entails *doing justice*. In an unjust world, shalom must include the attempt to put things right, acknowledging wrongs inflicted and seeking restoration. It includes a challenge to the oppressors and hope for the oppressed. It includes a liberation mandate that is concerned with the asymmetrical power structures dominating our world. Wolterstorff insists that Scripture makes it clear that

> the cries of the poor, of the oppressed, and of the victimized touch God's heart, and ... the groans of God's created but now polluted earth bring tears to God's eyes. If a college is to commit itself to serving the God of the Bible it must commit itself, as an academic institution, to serve the cause of justice in the world. I find no detour around this conclusion.[10]

This twin emphasis on social justice and ecological stewardship is at the core of CCSP's work in creation care and is encapsulated in the term *earth justice* we explore below. We desire to teach about and for justice so that our graduates practice justice.[11]

- Shalom will only be complete when we have "*delight* and *joy*" in our relationships with God, others, creation, and self.[12] It is not enough to be rid of violence and injustice. Only when there is enjoyment in who we are and in that with which we are in relationship, will shalom be fully realized. In these three ways shalom finds completeness.

Wolterstorff has argued extensively that merely communicating knowledge is inadequate for Christian education.[13] In earlier writings Wolterstorff focused on three teaching tools: reasoning, discipline, and modeling. However, an important shift in Wolterstorff's thinking has been the addition of a fourth factor: the cultivation of empathy for the world around us. We turn now to this additional factor, central to CCSP's pedagogy.

Wolterstorff suggests that although empathy is not typically cultivated in educational praxis, it is critical that educators actively seek to do so.

The most effective way to do this is by direct experience with victims of injustice:

> If people are to be energized to struggle to undo injustice, it is important that they listen to the voices and see the faces of the victims so that empathy can be invoked…. [R]eading books about injustice is, for most people, including myself, far less effective in energizing them to action than actually listening to the voices and actually seeing the faces of victims.[14]

Wolterstorff insists that the walls between school and life outside the classroom "must become much more porous than traditionally they have been" with teachers exploring ways "of bringing life into the classroom and of bringing the classroom to life."[15] Engaging in the world (and bringing the world into the classroom) is therefore one of Wolterstorff's key recommendations for leading students into empathetic and shalom-seeking relationships with the wounded world. With these convictions, Wolterstorff commends international study-abroad programs (for American students) to developing countries:

> We must try to give our students some sense of the interlocking structure of the modern world, and some sense of the impact of the West, particularly the United States, on the rest of the world. I am inclined to think that for one thing, a good many of our students must be involved in the Third World. Traditionally our foreign-study programs have been heavily oriented toward Europe; I think we must begin to achieve some balance here.[16]

While we fully embrace Wolterstorff's concept of empathy, we want to add two additional elements that are congruent with Wolterstorff's perspectives. First, although his work primarily addresses the need for empathy with suffering humans, we believe this should be extended to a wounded and suffering creation. Second, we also suggest that in stressed ecosystems, as within suffering individuals and communities, there may also be beauty and goodness to be apprehended and celebrated. This is an increasingly essential art.

Wolterstorff concludes that the implications of taking empathy seriously will be "appallingly radical for our teaching, for our living, and for the comportment of our institutions."[17] Indeed, for Wolterstorff shalom-centered education constitutes a third stage in the development of Christian higher education.[18] First-stage colleges trained young people in piety and evangelism, and the second broadened this out to cultural concerns. The third stage (which includes CCSP) adds three additional foci: (1) a greater sense of international consciousness; (2) new packaging of learning involving new disciplines, new ways of learning, and greater multidisciplinary engagement; and (3) greater concern "not just to understand the world but to change it."

We believe the following must characterize an education project that seeks to embody a shalom approach:

- *Faith-informed:* It must encourage and inspire faith in the living God. It will intentionally seek to challenge and broaden "childhood" faiths. A vibrant spirituality will be part of this; without it religion is breathless and education runs the risk of abstracting God from real-life experience.[19] CCSP has shaped a spiritual focus around "general sacramentality."[20]

- *Values and character:* Educating for shalom cannot be apolitical or amoral. Rather, our politics must reflect what Jim Wallis calls "God's politics."[21] The God of the Bible has given us the task to struggle for justice for the marginalized and the vulnerable.[22] Education cannot therefore be merely intellectual, though sharpening students' intellects has its place. The entire education institution must also embrace emotions, character-building, and life goals and priorities.

- *Engagement:* Brian Walsh suggests that the appropriate biblical categories of Christian faith are neither optimism nor pessimism but rather prophetic critique and prophetic hope.[23] The earth and its inhabitants have many wounds. A Christian education must address these wounds and the reasons they exist. However, it must also articulate hope in the redeeming power of a God who calls us to respond by imagining and pursuing alternatives.

By placing the shalom model at the heart of our work, CCSP intentionally pursues a radical educational project. We seek to align our entire pedagogy with this goal. Our discussion below details some of the ways we have carried out this mission of shalom. Before we continue, however, we have two qualifiers. First, ours is not the only way; we can imagine a variety of other ways in which shalom could be made central to an educational project.[24] Second, we know that our attempt at a shalom-centered education is an incomplete and sometimes flawed work in progress. All attempts at such a high ideal will be met by disappointments on some, if not most, fronts. Nevertheless, we want to present CCSP as one example of an educational project that is actively seeking to do shalom in education.

On Believing in an Earthy Faith

Our reading of shalom, and consequently the focus of our educational praxis, is that we should seek to inspire in students a thoroughly earthy faith. We have found the concept of earthiness a useful rubric through which to explore the implications of the gospel. We believe that it is becoming increasingly critical that Christians of all hues, and perhaps evangelicals in particular, recover an earthy faith – a faith at home in this world, a faith that perceives God working in this place, and a faith that works for the redemption of all creation. This is not simply plucking survivors from a sinking ship, but rather participation in God's work of restoring the entire boat.

Much has been written on the necessity of an earthy faith, but we must necessarily be brief.[25] The context of this call to an earthy faith is the crisis of (un)sustainability and ecological degradation facing our societies today and the ambivalence, at best, of the Christian church. Questions of environmental degradation are made all the more pressing given the fact that their effects are disproportionately borne by the poor and marginalized. There is therefore a critical need for a radical change in our relationship with the earth. The onus rests on us to reorient ourselves so that the earth is cherished rather than exploited.

Despite the ambivalence of the Christian church toward this issue, there exists within the Christian faith, and the biblical text, the resources for a response. We agree with Bouma-Prediger when he writes, "The gospel is surely more than caring for the earth, but just as surely it involves nothing less."[26]

A central aspect of an earthy faith is an affirmation of the physical, material, and embodied; to affirm that "matter matters."[27] This affirmation is founded on Christology: Christ's life (the incarnation of God on this earth), death (the power of God's love for the whole earth), resurrection (the eschatological hope in Christ for the earth), and reign (the rule of Christ over the whole earth).[28] It also draws upon the centrality of the earth (or "land") within Old Testament narratives.[29] An earthy faith sees humanity in intimate relationship with the earth. Rasmussen puts it thus: "Earth is bone of our bone and flesh of our flesh."[30] This acknowledgment is critical. No longer can we see ourselves separated from the earth. Instead, we are completely dependent upon, and interrelated with, the earth.

An earthy faith finds expression in a vibrant *sacramentalist spirituality* that makes space in our worship of God for our relationships of belonging to the earth. This sacramentalist perspective seeks to recover a vision of Christ in our neighbors, especially the poor and marginalized. It also acknowledges that only on this earth can we, as embodied persons, see, feel, touch, and sense the presence of God. But it is not only humanity: all creation exists to voice worship to the Creator.[31] Sacramentalist spirituality enables a reimagining of the world in which we can see fingerprints of the Creator God in creation around us. An earthy faith will also express itself through a desire to seek an *earth justice*, a justice that combines social justice and ecological stewardship in a desire to see shalom restored to all creation.

A sacramentalist spirituality and an earth justice are critical for – and necessary expressions of – an earthy faith. They are also related to empathy. A sacramentalist spirituality feeds into empathy through a reimagining of the world. One feels empathy for creation through seeing God's imprint in creation. Without an empathetic, emotional bond and a sense of urgency the struggle for justice will never be entertained, and an earthy faith is hollow. Teaching for an earthy faith that pursues shalom will therefore situate the building of these empathetic relationships at the center of its pedagogy. As Bouma-Prediger makes clear, however, "We care for only what we love. We love only what we know. We truly know only what we experience."[32] This linking of love, knowledge, and experience echoes Wolterstorff's emphasis on the need for direct experience and also preempts our discussion of ecological literacy in the section that follows. Thus, together with sacramentalist spirituality and earth justice, empathy is at the heart of an earthy faith.

On Being Ecologically Literate

David Orr is perhaps the foremost theorist on education and the environment. Passionate and defiant, Orr challenges his readers to think hard about both the educational status quo and alternatives that inspire treasuring the earth. Orr advocates an education *on* and *for* the environment. We reflect here on some of Orr's insights as these have informed CCSP's work and pedagogy.

At the heart of Orr's understanding of the contemporary environmental crisis is that it is primarily a spiritual crisis: "Increasingly children grow up in a thoroughly secular culture, often without awareness that life is both gift and mystery. They are, in other words, spiritually impoverished."[33] This has led to an undervaluing of life, which in turn has opened up the misuse and abuse of the environment and each other. The spiritual crisis has been precipitated and shaped by a crisis of "mind, perception, and values";[34] that is, a crisis of education. Orr argues that the spiritual vacuity of our education has meant that it has been complicit in a sustained attack on nature and in the production of an unsustainable society.

In the face of a crisis of education, Orr calls for a rethinking of the way we do education in the hope that educational institutions will become "leverage points for the transition to sustainability."[35] He calls for an "ecological literacy" that will involve "breaking free of old pedagogical assumptions, of the straightjacket of the discipline-centered curriculum, and even of confinement in classrooms and school buildings."[36] An ecologically literate education centers on the question "What will people need to know to live responsibly and well in a finite world?"[37] Orr's response is that an ecological education must include "knowing, caring and practical competency."[38] This three-way connection among knowledge/understanding, values/priorities, and tangible concrete tools is vital. Like Wolterstorff, Orr insists that a merely intellectual education will not suffice. Instead, we must seek to ensure our graduates are people who can think intelligently and critically about the issues affecting the world today, are deeply concerned with the wounds of the world, and can translate knowledge and concern into action.

In Orr's discussion of ecological literacy, CCSP has found a pedagogical home. We affirm and incorporate Orr's six key foundations for ecological literacy into the running of our program. Here, however, there is only space to address one: the critical nature of direct experience.[39] A central aspect of Orr's critique of the education status quo is that it is too isolated from the world. He mourns the pedagogical disaster of students "shut off from the natural world, sealed in a cocoon of steel, glass, and concrete, enveloped in a fog of mind-debilitating electronic pulsations."[40] From this, Orr proposes a "jail break" that would take learners out of the classroom far more often.[41] In his writings Orr suggests that there are at least five reasons necessitating direct experience/field education:

- *Affinity or empathy:* Orr calls for creating an emotional bond between ourselves and nature because we will not fight for what we do not love;[42]
- *Good thinking:* Experience of the natural world is an "antidote to indoor, abstract learning" and therefore essential to good thinking;[43]
- *Sacredness of life:* Only through experiencing nature can we form a reverence for life;[44]
- *Anti-consumerism:* "Capitalism works best when children stay indoors in malls and in front of televisions or computer screens. It loses its access to the minds of the young when they discover pleasures that cannot be bought";[45] and
- *Practical learning:* "A genuinely liberal education will also connect the head and the hands" – this can only be done by giving hands a chance to work, feel, touch, and experience.[46]

We hear Orr's voice as prophetic, calling education to a higher ethical place. While we would not want to present the division between classroom and field quite as sharply as Orr is polemically prone to do (we continue to see the classroom space as an important learning tool), we also suggest that the reasons Orr gives for valuing field education ring true and his "jail break" from exclusively indoor pedagogies is well overdue.

On Being Subversively "Out of the Box"

As Brian Walsh and Sylvia Keesmaat argue, an authentic expression of Christianity will necessarily be subversive.[47] The empires of this world will always be in conflict with the kingdom of God. We understand subversion as having two interrelated meanings:

- *Challenges the powers:* Subversion involves an intentional critiquing of the powers that be. The profound discontinuity between our present society and the vision of shalom (that is, the nature of God's kingdom) cannot be avoided. Walsh argues that authentic Christianity is "deeply offensive to the dominant forces in our culture." He continues:

  > A Christian worldview, a Christian lifestyle lived in the light of the events of Easter, proclaims that the true lord of history is the crucified and risen one – the one who proclaimed that the kingdom of God is at hand. And that kingdom, that rule, undermines all other pretentious kingdoms and all other cultural experiments that are not rooted in the kingdom of God. This kingdom calls for their total redirection. This is a gospel that is subversive and therefore, for those who benefit from present socio-cultural arrangements, offensive.[48]

- *Gets under the skin:* Subversion is not always direct conflict. Rather it is often lateral, subtle, cryptic, oblique. Subversion, in this second sense, is when the message *gets under the skin* before the full power explodes.

We argue that Christian education, especially pursing a shalom model, will be subversive in intent.[49] We must lead our students in critiquing and even actively undermining the "powers" that stand in contention with the kingdom of God. Of course, we must also assert alternatives; these will also take on a subversive power in challenging the status quo and demanding new priorities and structures. We also need to be intelligent and thoughtful in our approach. The proverbial soapbox is all too easily ignored or inspires knee-jerk us-versus-them reactions. We need to explore ways to get under the skin of our students – to present the power and profound nature of the gospel in ways that will infuse their whole being – and get behind the socio-psychological walls that we all construct to protect ourselves. At CCSP we have sought to engage in a subversive education that challenges the powers and gets under the skin of our students, primarily through an "out-of-the-box" pedagogy.

The phrase "out-of-the-box education" captures two aspects of CCSP's pedagogy. First, "box" stands for the norms of tertiary education. We seek to push beyond these norms in a creative educational praxis. The box is not done away with altogether, but we have sought to conceptualize a very different box such that all the boundaries have been pushed and the walls are far more fluid. Second, the "box" refers to the physical walls and pedagogical spaces of classroom learning. We seek to escape this second box through field-intensive study abroad. Again, the classroom walls are not dispensed with altogether. All our courses employ the classroom as a useful educational space. However, we question why so much education is limited to this claustrophobic space. Why keep the world so distant from our education? We also argue – again drawing on Wolterstorff and Orr – that direct experience is key to building empathy.

Believing and Being with CCSP Belize

In the sections above we have articulated the philosophical infrastructure upon which CCSP has grounded its pedagogy. We now turn to see how these ideas have informed our educational praxis. We first provide further background information and then discuss our pedagogical approach.

Creation Care Study Program runs two university-level, semester-long study-abroad programs: one in Belize, Central America, and the other in the South Pacific (New Zealand and Samoa). Between ten and twenty students each semester per program undergo an intense, academically rigorous, field-based education taught in consecutive block courses. For most of the semester, students reside in a campus-like setting. CCSP began in 2002, though its leadership has strong and lengthy backgrounds in both study abroad and field education. For present purposes, we focus on the Belize program.

Institutionally, CCSP has several distinctive characteristics which assist in creating space for exploring alternative pedagogies:

- *Young organization:* CCSP has operated for only four years and is still very much in the process of learning the way forward. It is not yet, therefore, in a rigid mold. We are willing to trial new structures, new curricula, new combinations, and new systems to see what works.

- *Distinctive focus:* CCSP is the only semester-length study-abroad program offered within North American Christian higher education with a direct and pervasive emphasis on issues of creation care.
- *Orbits the Christian academy:* CCSP is both an "insider" and "outsider" to the North American Christian academy. We have drawn from, but are not constrained by, these institutions.
- *Flexibility:* Although accountable to supporting institutions,[50] CCSP is nevertheless a small, independent, and organizationally flat institution with the ability to change and adapt quickly, both institutionally and pedagogically.
- *Self-reflexivity:* CCSP cultivates an intentionally self-reflexive approach for each activity we carry out.

CCSP Belize students take three core courses: God and Nature, Sustainable Community Development, and Tropical Ecosystems.[51] Although each course has its own distinct focus – theology, social justice, and ecology respectively – there are also significant interconnections. These interactions help students create bridges between different disciplines and provide a more holistic focus for creation care. The three core courses, combined with an internship elective (during which students work with local organizations), constitute the majority of facilitated educational experience each semester.

Being Field Intensive

Why study in Belize? So that Belize can become the classroom. We come *to* Belize to learn *from* Belize. Of course, another possible response to the same question would be similar to that given by the thousands of tourists who visit Belize each year: the cayes are beautiful, the barrier reef is amazing, the Mayan archeological sites are awe-inspiring, the rainforest is stunning, the cultures are fascinating. These are answers that many of our students would be inclined to give, and it is precisely here that study abroad and field education is subversive.[52] That which is desired – beauty, otherness, adventure – can be used to facilitate a response more radical than the tourist's fleeting glimpse. Being present in Belize can help create empathy with those living in this part of the developing world and with a beautiful but increasingly stressed environment. Studying abroad in such a context can also provide a "cultural detox": separation from one's home society, so much of which revolves around hyper-consumption, can allow a critical distance that enables deeper self-reflexivity.

Good fieldtrips, in our thinking, enable students to engage with Belizean realities, inspire empathy, and help motivate an earthy faith. As we have learned through both successes and failures, good fieldtrips have the following qualities:

- *Balance:* Each course is a four-way balance among field experience, classroom learning, reading/assignment time, and free time. Rather than rigid rules, the four elements are combined in different ways depending on (a) type and requirements of each specific course, (b) preferences of faculty, (c) the relation between different courses within the context of the semester, and (d) students' level of energy.
- *Strategic, illustrative and appropriate:* It would be impossible to visit the whole of Belize, and attempting to do so would result in a poor place-based education. Instead, we create detailed itineraries that suit the specifics of each course so that every fieldtrip fits within an overall conceptual framework. This can only be done well with detailed knowledge of the Belizean context. Each fieldtrip is designed to illustrate material that is explored in class time and readings;
- *Clearly conceptualized:* Effective fieldtrips are clearly and carefully introduced with the purpose of the trip and the intended connections with the rest of the course clearly articulated. Likewise, a thorough debrief is necessary;
- *Assessment:* We find that academic fieldtrips work best when there is a specific assessment or task required as part of the fieldtrip. This encourages engagement and facilitates a deeper processing of the experience.

Good fieldtrips also facilitate new ways of perceiving the world. An effective fieldtrip involves a shift in the students' imagination. We summarize our emphasis on perception in the following two points:

- *Seeing deeply:* In everyday life people tend to see quite superficially, but a good academic education will always facilitate new ways of looking at things such that the multiple layers of meaning that constitute the world around us become visible and students are given the tools to discern meaning in the midst of complexity.
- *Interconnectedness:* This has two senses. First, interconnectedness refers to how all spheres of life are tied together, and therefore our analysis in each field context needs to strive to be holistic. Second, it refers to how in a globalized world all societies are connected with each other.

These two processes will serve to focus our discussion of the two case studies below.

Academic courses are not the sole engagement in the field. Various other experiential activities are facilitated each semester that are not part of formal academic classes, including field experiences for orientation and debrief weeks, cultural fieldtrips, and worship activities. In addition, students' own explorations of Belize in their free time are an important part of their learning. Though we do not analyze these not-for-credit activities here, it is important to note the critical role they play. They represent our commitment to working beyond the spatial and temporal boundaries of normal education, too much of which begins and ends in a formal educational (classroom) space. These experiences can be influential in forming student responses to the theme of an earthy faith. The experiential activities that CCSP staff facilitate often create opportunities for open dialogue with and among students unmediated by the constraints of academic spaces. These conversations and relationships are more open to including and engaging with the emotional, which is a critical component of an empathetic response to the wounds of the world and also of the desire to seek alternatives. These experiential activities are therefore a key part of CCSP's work.

In the following section we address the formal academic field experiences involved in the program. Rather than provide a comprehensive list of academic fieldtrips, we outline two case studies as representative examples. Each example has been chosen because it provides insight into the "out-of-the-box" and "subversive" education that we provide in our attempts to ground students in an earthy faith. The first fieldtrip involves a visit to Cockscomb Basin Wildlife Sanctuary for the forest ecology component of Tropical Ecology. The second is a visit to the village of Patchakan, Corozal District for Sustainable Community Development. Both descriptions are based primarily on the spring 2005 semester. The case studies are structured around and help illustrate how "seeing deeply" and perceiving "interconnectedness" are critical to reimagining the world through experiential education.

Tropical Forest Ecology at Cockscomb Basin Wildlife Sanctuary

Each ecology course we operate at CCSP Belize is immersed in the field. Visiting the rainforest in Belize is not difficult. However, a brief visit can leave one bewildered and lost. The rainforest is a complex and mysterious ecosystem that requires careful teaching to explain it to the untrained eye.

Our visit to Cockscomb Basin Wildlife Sanctuary (CBWS) is very much the centerpiece for the forest ecology class.[53] Created in 1986 because of the high numbers of jaguar found in the basin, the 128,000 acres of CBWS are also home to a rich range of flora and fauna.[54] However, it is not untouched by human contact. The park headquarters were formerly a logging camp, and much of the old growth mahogany and other valuable timber have been extracted by a succession of logging operations. This, combined with a direct hit from Hurricane Hattie in 1961, has meant that much of the forest is secondary growth.[55] However, vegetation grows quickly in the tropics, and the forest has made strong recovery from natural and human destruction alike.

From an ecological as well as a conservation perspective, CBWS is an ideal site to visit when studying tropical forest ecology. Although sightings of mammals are notoriously difficult in the rainforest (it is definitely *not* a zoo), in our four-day, three-night stay we invariably sight a range of mammal, amphibian, bird, and reptile life. Whereas animal life can be unpredictable and shy, the thick and diverse flora surrounds us. Dave Warners, a biology professor at Calvin College and CCSP Belize's faculty for Forest Ecology for spring 2005, led numerous excursions while at CBWS. Trail hiking, early-morning birding, and night hikes were all daily experiences.

While hiking a track, Dave pulls to one side and gathers us together. Using a plant specimen located at the side of the track, Dave lectures on what the students see. He highlights the ways in which each element in the forest ecosystem is interconnected with others. Students respond with questions and scribble furiously in their field notebooks. Mosquitoes biting our ankles and necks, cicadas chirping hypnotically around us, sweat beading on our foreheads – this seems an odd place for a classroom. Yet this is a profound learning environment. Assisted by reading (Kricher's invaluable *Neotropical Companion*[56] and other articles) and lectures before and after the experience, students who previously knew little about neotropical flora and fauna are quick to grasp Dave's field observations. As Dave discusses with the students what they are seeing, they receive new lenses through which to look at the rainforest. First impressions of a messy, unordered, chaotic, and incomprehensible tangle of green give way to a new understanding of order and identifiable distinctions. Although it is impossible to fully understand the complex processes that take place here, by looking deeper we gain a greater appreciation of the complex interactions occurring in this ecosystem.

The seeing deeper also comes from guest speakers and informal conversations. CBWS wardens, many of whom are Mopan Maya living in buffer-zone communities and some of whom have worked at CBWS since its inception almost 20 years ago, are invaluable sources of knowledge about local fauna and flora, the nearby village communities, and ongoing conservation efforts. With this in mind, we invite Ernesto Saqui to talk with our students about the history of the park and plans for the future. Ernesto, a Mopan Maya, is the former director of CBWS and is passionate for his people and for the park. Ernesto explains that when the park was formed, the Maya living at Quam Bank (near the current park headquarters) were simply ordered to leave with no explanation or compensation. Understandably, this created a feeling of bitterness among the buffer zone communities. However, Ernesto and others have since worked closely with the Maya communities to create a system in which both the communities and CBWS can benefit. The intention is for management of the park to be eventually handed over to the buffer zone communities (currently it is managed by the Belize Audubon Society). Both the material benefits from tourism and a growing sense of concern for the wildlife in the basin, inspired in part by CBWS public education programs, have led to a greater sense of appreciation for the sanctuary in recent years. Ernesto also addresses the current challenges CBWS faces, including the perennial issue of funding and questions as to the tourist carrying capacity of the park and facilities. Later, other wardens complain of tourists carelessly throwing plastic wrappers at the side of tracks and the time-consuming process of cleaning up after them. Clearly, tourists can be both blessing and curse.

Ernesto's wife, Aurora Saqui (one of the famous Garcia Sisters), also addresses our group on questions of ethnobotany and traditional Maya healing practices. Aurora explains how Maya use many different plants for a whole range of ailments. She shows that humanity is deeply connected with the forest. Conservation is not just for nature's sake.

Visiting researchers from the United Kingdom, Bart and Becky, also facilitate deeper sight. None of us have seen a jaguar during our stay at CBWS, but that doesn't reduce our interest in their presentations on these shy cats. Bart discusses his doctoral research on jaguars at CBWS. Students are glued to his work as he exhibits hundreds of photographs of jaguars taken from motion-sensor cameras. Bart identifies each one by their unique spot patterns. He also explains his research methodology and praxis. Becky discusses her research into "problem jaguars" – jaguars that venture close to human settlements and feed off livestock and other domestic animals. She shares her insights into the challenges and opportunities for supporting jaguar conservation in Belize.

We see that we have seen so little. The rainforest remains a deep mystery. We see also the sort of work that takes place in order to research the creatures that live in the rainforest. Biology students are inspired and the rest of us feel deep respect. We also see again that each conservation endeavor is never in isolation. There are no fences around this sanctuary keeping the wildlife in and humans out. It is insufficient to merely protect nature without thinking also of the human dimensions of conservation – the two are always interconnected.

Each part of the CBWS fieldtrip contributes to helping us see much deeper. By experiencing and interacting with CBWS ecosystems and those who are passionate about its conservation, we are given an invitation to celebrate it, enjoy it, and care for it. We leave with memories of beautiful scenery, deep and ongoing challenges, hope, and a profound admiration for both the ecology of the park and the people who work there.

Sustainable Community Development at Patchakan

Patchakan is a small rural village located in the Corozal District near the border of Belize and Mexico. The professor for the spring 2005 visit to Patchakan was Gail Heffner, also from Calvin College, who wove an analysis of food systems throughout her course. Gail was active throughout the class, provoking questions and drawing (inter-)connections.

A Maya/Mestizo town, the people of Patchakan primarily speak Spanish, and some know little or no English (the official language of Belize). Houses vary in size and quality. Some are made of concrete with running water for showers and have electric refrigerators and gas stoves. Others are constructed from locally gathered timber and have thatch roofs, no running water, no electricity, a pit latrine, and an open fireplace for cooking. All the households would be regarded as being in a state of poverty had they been located in the United States or Canada. However, no one from Patchakan has ever described themselves as being poor during our visits. These houses are their homes, constructed by their hard work and kept going by their dedication. They raise their families here, and love, hope, and faith are expressed here just as in any other place.

Traditionally, the villagers would have been primarily subsistence *milpa* farmers. However, sugarcane is now virtually a monocrop in Patchakan, and many families rely heavily or exclusively on the crop for their livelihood. Sugarcane growing in Belize has a substantial, if varied, history.[57] The first sugarcane cuttings were introduced here in the 1840s. Up until the 1950s, sugarcane was cultivated primarily in large-scale plantations. However, from the 1950s on, small-scale Maya and Mestizo farmers became the main growers of the crop, and in Patchakan sugarcane eventually replaced *milpa* farming. The history of sugarcane cultivation is characterized by boom and bust cycles associated with changes in international trade (only a small proportion of sugar is cultivated for the local market).[58] Currently, Belize appears to be on a long spiral toward bust. Threatened by increased global competition and the decline of guaranteed preferential access associated with calls for free trade, Patchakan's sugarcane farmers over the past decade have received less and less return from their labor.

The decline of the sugar industry has seen a variety of alternatives open up:

- The Commercial Free Zone (CFZ) is located between the Belizean and Mexican customs and immigration offices. Designed after the Panama model, this government-led initiative provides consumer products exclusively to non-Belizeans (primarily Mexicans) at exceptionally low tax rates. The CFZ provides employment to Belizeans, including a number of young men and women from Patchakan.
- Papaya farms, primarily exporting to North America, have also been initiated in the last decade. Men from the village of Patchakan work on these farms in manual labor tasks. Due to high initial setup costs, operating a commercially viable papaya plantation is out of the reach of most Belizeans.
- Tourism, the largest industry in terms of foreign exchange earnings in the Belizean economy, also contributes extensively to the Corozal district. However, few tourists – with the exception of a large number of short-term mission trips each summer – come to Patchakan. Even the short-term missioners tend to stay in the town of Corozal rather than Patchakan itself. Again, with the exception of being employed by someone else in the industry, there are few opportunities here for the villagers of Patchakan.

Patchakan is a small village shaped and reshaped by the whims of the global economy. Currently, Patchakan's alternatives to a declining sugar industry are mostly limited to unskilled and poorly paid labor in other export-oriented industries. This serves to further exacerbate the villagers' vulnerability.

Our fieldtrip starts early in the morning with a three-hour bus ride from Nabitunich, our campus, to Corozal District. Our first stop is the Belize Sugar Industry factory at Tower Hill. A guide has been arranged to show us around. Arriving at the factory, we are immediately struck by row upon row of trucks, each piled to overflowing with sugarcane, lined up as far as we can see: a larger-than-life conveyor belt. The factory – complete with smoking stacks, large corrugated iron warehouses, sounds of cranks and steaming water, men standing around in hard hats, and machines of various shapes and enormous sizes – is also quite a sight. Ash from the smoke stacks sticks to our sweaty skin. The smell of sweet burning fills our nostrils. The tour takes two hours, during which we walk around the entire factory viewing various aspects of production. The sugarcane comes from about 8000 independent farmers and is processed and exported primarily to Europe and the United States. We learn of the various international pressures that have pushed down the financial returns.[59] We also learn that although the United States heavily protects its own sugar beet industry, it insists that others liberalize their economies. We also see the piles of waste pulp left in huge heaps at the rear of the complex. We learn that every industry produces waste. Finally, before we leave, we see raw sugar granules piled in enormous pyramids, each three stories high. We learn that the trade agreements our countries push for, as well as our consumption patterns and lifestyles inform and impact the Belizean economy.

Having seen where sugarcane is delivered, it is time to see where it comes from. We arrive in Patchakan in the early afternoon and meet Alfonso Vallejos at the local Presbyterian church. Alfonso is our gatekeeper for our time in Patchakan. Quietly spoken and a true gentleman, Alfonso is the primary reason we keep returning to Patchakan. Alfonso has previously worked as a Christian Reformed World Relief Committee extension worker and has also served in the Cane Farmers' Association. His perspective combines intimately local knowledge, a solid understanding of the wider issues, and a thoroughly Christian sense of compassion for his village.

Alfonso talks with us about Patchakan's history, politics, economics, culture, and future prospects. Focusing on the sugar industry, his words are both inspiring and discouraging. Alfonso describes the declining sugar industry as an oncoming hurricane: although maybe still a few days off, the disaster is coming, and Patchakan is unprepared. All too soon sugarcane will cease to be viable for the small farmer, with input costs (fertilizer, labor, transport, etc.) increasing and profit margins declining. Already many farmers are acquiring significant debt and investors are forming larger plantations in order to increase competitiveness. These processes are forcing the small farmer out of sugarcane farming altogether. The village, however, remains totally unprepared for the impending shifts. We learn again that what we serve on our tables back home affects the livelihoods of people who depend on it.

Alfonso also articulates his dream: a study farm that would revive the traditional *milpa* farming practices which have mostly been forgotten in the past five decades and introduce new techniques and plant varieties. The economic changes over recent generations have impacted what cultural knowledge was maintained and what was ignored. Alfonso has gathered a group of people who are interested in the dream, and he has made some of his own land available. The farm is designed to serve as an example to others on how to provide for themselves and for the local market. Alfonso's faith in a fickle global economy is weak at best. He dreams of his neighbors diversifying their agriculture and creating a more stable and sure local economy. His dream inspires and challenges.

Later that same afternoon we visit the Patchakan Presbyterian mission clinic. This foreign-run and predominantly foreign-financed operation is one of the best-stocked clinics in the country. We are addressed by clinic staff who talk to us about significant causes of ill health in the village.[60] We learn how health, the economy, and the environment are all interrelated. Almost all the medical and administrative staff come from the United States. We learn that churches in the States – similar to our own – impact Patchakan in a variety of important ways.

At the end of a long day we are distributed to our homestay families. Alfonso places some of us in People's United Party homes and some in United Democratic Party homes.[61] He also places our students with Roman Catholic, Pentecostal, and Presbyterian families. Alfonso uses our group to help cut across the lines that divide his community (political and religious). He believes that unity will be one of the most important things to foster in the challenges ahead. We learn that some of the divisions experienced and originating in our societies also impact Patchakan. We also learn of the importance of community in addressing economic issues and concerns.

That evening some of us watch television in Spanish with our host families: Disney cartoons, Hollywood sitcoms, Mexican soap operas. Many families are glued to the television until it is time to sleep. We learn that the entertainment that our societies produce is beamed into the homes of people in Patchakan. We also engage in conversations on all sorts of topics – family, work, faith, politics, food – learning about our host families and sharing about our own.

The next day our first classroom is Alfonso's sugarcane field. He talks with us about soil quality (diminishing), rainfall (exceptionally low for the season and, apparently, also diminishing), nitrogen fixation, and the various sugarcane varieties and their uses. We get sunburned. While munching on some of Alfonso's sugarcane we learn about the interconnections between agriculture and the environment. Later we check out Alfonso's study farm and see the crops he is growing and the irrigation system he is hoping to set up. We learn of the various challenges he faces and the people who have agreed to work with him. We learn of the help he has received from various donors – mostly from the United States. Our knowledge of the sugarcane industry, and of Alfonso's alternative, is deepened.

Mid-morning we drive out of Patchakan to visit a papaya plantation owned by a company from the United States. The manager gives us a tour around this example of industrialized agriculture. He tells us that the fungicides they spray on the papaya are banned in the United States. He tells us of the lowering water table due to overconsumption of water and consequently the need for deeper wells for the irrigation. He tells us that the papaya are destined for supermarkets in the United States. He assures us that there is no long-term impact on the land used for cultivation. However, he also says that they only rent land, and when they start receiving diminished yields they move on to a different site. He informs us that the company is a recipient of USAID funding. We see row upon row of papaya trees and learn again that our society's consumption patterns affect Patchakan.

The afternoon is easier going. After reading and discussion, we go back to our host families and spend the rest of the evening with them: mostly again watching television in Spanish. Some of the families tell us that we are different from most other foreign visitors they have met because we stay with local families and share in their daily lives. We also contribute to their livelihoods.

Through directly experiencing life in Patchkan, we can see in tangible ways how our lives are interrelated with theirs through trade, consumption, environment, culture, and politics. The recognition of these interconnections brings a greater onus to consider our society's own economics and politics. Crucially, our visit enables us to *feel* for those in Patchakan; their hopes, fears, livelihoods, opportunities, and constraints are no longer abstract intellectual constructs but have become grounded in the real lives of the people we have met.

Conclusion

These two examples ground our discussion in concrete experience of actual field activities. We have used the concepts of "seeing deeply" and "interconnectedness" throughout to highlight the value of direct experience, which can create a space for empathy. Although field education is never simple or straightforward, it is nevertheless invaluable for teaching on and for social justice and ecological stewardship.

This paper has presented CCSP Belize as a case study in being and believing. Building upon Wolterstorff's "shalom" model of Christian education, an understanding of the gospel requiring an earthy faith, and Orr's call for "ecological literacy," we have argued that *being there* (through study abroad and field education) is a powerful and subversive pedagogical practice that can be used to help inspire belief; that is, an earthy faith. More specifically, we have shown how we have incorporated a strong focus on building empathy into our educational practice through field-based experiences. This has been done in order to inspire students toward an earth justice that includes a sacramentalist spirituality that seeks to re-imagine the world in a more mystical light.

The current dominant models of education tend to employ an exclusively classroom-based pedagogy. This spatial and experiential limitation artificially cuts students off from a range of rich learning contexts outside the classroom. More importantly, a Christian education that seeks to be not merely an intellectual pursuit, but one that also promotes faith, values, and engagement, will be deeply concerned with building empathy in our students. The best (though not the only) way to build empathy is through direct experience. Wolterstorff and Orr agree on this point; our educational practice should work "out of the box." They also agree that empathy is a crucial virtue that we need to inspire in our students in order to encourage them to work toward positive change in the world today.

The above discussion raises a pragmatic question: Can CCSP's model of placing "being there" back at the center of its education be replicated by other Christian educational institutions? Or put another way: Is it practical for all Christian educational institutions to seek to work beyond the confines of the classroom in their education practice? We answer this question by looking at both elements of our "being there": field experience and study abroad.

- *Field experience:* The "field" need not be conceptualized as being at the other side of the world. There is a certain value, as we discuss below, in going overseas to developing countries, but it is essential that this not be the beginning or end for field education. An effective and profound "jail break" can be as close as the nearest forest park, a neighborhood retirement home, a local soup kitchen, a particular ethnic club in the community, an organization working on racial reconciliation, a food co-op practicing an alternative politics of consumption, a local eco-farm, an international development organization's office, a local artist who imagines a new world, a fair trade café, the nearest prison, an inner city church engaged in care for the homeless, or an indigenous community engaging in issues of compensation for wrongs inflicted on it. This brief list hints at the endless opportunities for field experiences that many of us could easily find in our own local communities.

- *Study abroad:* More university-level students should certainly be encouraged to study abroad in developing countries. The need to understand in a more comprehensive way the issues and challenges that face the majority world is critical. Students from the West need to know that the way their societies do their politics, economics, and consumption directly impacts those living elsewhere. Students also need to be encouraged to feel empathy for people in other parts of the world, in the hope that this compassion will inform the way they live their lives. However, study abroad isn't the only way to get there. More young people should be encouraged to undertake voluntary work overseas. This is not the same thing as the highly popular "short term mission" trips that, in our minds, are generally inadequate to the task. The period of time must be longer and the experience focused more intentionally toward opening students' minds and subverting students' preconceptions.

Field experience can and should be a part of our everyday curricula. Study-abroad programs like CCSP Belize can play a key part in students' lives by creating space for empathic relationships, but they should never be considered adequate in and of themselves. We believe that a shalom model of education and the pressing need to encourage students toward an earthy faith should be something that all Christian educational institutions should strive for. If an institution accepts this position, it will necessarily seek to immerse students in the messy world in which we live through direct experience.

Many of our students' trajectories have been challenged and sometimes transformed as part of their involvement in CCSP. However, the level of change has been different in each individual, with no one student's metamorphosis identical to another's. Change has taken place in all our students, though not always in the ways we had intended. This is something we cherish. Our goal is to help students be a part of God's work in this world. We hope that students will pick up and draw upon an ethic of ecological stewardship and social justice in their everyday life; but to be an authentic expression of faith it must come from within them. We can only help create the space in which such an ethic could be planted; whether it will come to fruition or not is something over which we have little control. Nevertheless, the value of this education is in providing the opportunities and impetus for our students to mature into Christians who will work for shalom in their daily lives. Being there is a critical variable in believing, and Christian educational programs should seek to be there far more often.

Notes

1   We would like to thank Iris Lee and Tricia O'Connor Elisara for their helpful and insightful comments. CCSP staff and faculty have also provided invaluable insights which have directly shaped this paper. We are indebted to their

passion and dedication. We also thank the three anonymous reviewers for their comments. Any faults in the paper remain entirely our own.

2   See particularly: Wolterstorff, Nicholas, *Educating for Life: Reflections on Christian Teaching and Learning*, ed. Gloria Goris Stronks & Clarence W. Joldersma (Grand Rapids, MI: Baker Academic, 2002); and Wolterstorff, Nicholas, *Educating for Shalom: Essays on Christian Higher Education*, ed. Clarence W. Joldersma & Gloria Goris Stronks (Grand Rapids, MI: Baker Academic, 2004).

3   On the connection between the concept of earth as home and education see Bouma-Prediger, Steven, & Brian J. Walsh, "Education for Homelessness or Homemaking? The Christian College in a Postmodern Culture," in *Christian Scholars Review*, 32:3 (Spring 2003) pp. 281-295.

4   In addition to drawing from the two recent compilations of Wolterstorff's (2002, 2004) work on Christian education, we have also utilized Wolterstorff, Nicholas, *Until Justice and Peace Embrace* (Grand Rapids, MI: Eerdmans, 1983).

5   Wolterstorff (2004) p. 26.

6   Wolterstorff (2002) p. 262.

7   Wolterstorff (1983) p. 69.

8   Noll, Mark, *The Scandal of the Evangelical Mind* (Grand Rapids, MI: Eerdmans, 1995) pp. 51-56.

9   Wolterstorff (2004) p. 141.

10   Wolterstorff (2004) p. 25.

11   Wolterstorff (2004) p. 24.

12   Wolterstorff (1983) p. 124.

13   Wolterstorff (2002 & 2004).

14   Wolterstorff (2002) pp. 282-283.

15   Wolterstorff (2002) p. 139.

16   Wolterstorff (2004) p. 167.

17   Wolterstorff (2004) p. 152.

18   Wolterstorff (2004) pp. 33-34.

19   As Liberation theologian Leonardo Boff has argued: "A theology – any theology – not based on a spiritual experience is mere panting – religious breathlessness." Boff, Leonardo, "Salvation in Liberation: The Theological Meaning of Socio-historical Liberation" in Boff, Leonardo & Clodovis Boff, *Salvation and Liberation: In Search of a Balance Between Faith and Politics* (Maryknoll, NY: Orbis Books, 1979) p. 2.

20   Rockell, Brenda, "Ritual, Church and World: Building Up the Body of Christ, Connecting with the Culture Beyond the Church" (Unpublished manuscript, Auckland, New Zealand, 2005).

21   Wallis, Jim, *God's Politics: Why the Right Gets It Wrong and the Left Doesn't Get It*, (New York: HarperSanFrancisco, 2005).

22   On the inherently political nature of the gospel see also especially: Yoder, John Howard *The Politics of Jesus*, (Grand Rapids, MI: Eerdmans,1972) and Myers, Ched, *Binding the Strong Man: A Political Reading of Mark's Story of Jesus*, (New York: Orbis Books, 1988).

23   Walsh, Brian, *Subversive Christianity: Imaging God in a Dangerous Time* (Seattle, WA: Alta Vista College Press, 1992) p. 45.

24   Indeed, we believe that limiting a discussion of "Christian education" to just institutions that claim an explicit Christian identity is both problematic and mistaken as it ignores the work of Christian educators in the "secular" world. Chris Anderson's powerful and moving articulation of faith in the secular university should, we think, come as a challenge to us all not to exist merely in some form of private Christian club but to affirm that the church and Christian educators need the secular university, just as the secular university needs the Christian church. We have certainly gained much, personally and institutionally, from our engagement with "secular" education. See Anderson, Chris, *Teaching as Believing: Faith in the University* (Waco, TX: Baylor Univ. Press, 2004).

25   We draw here primarily on the following two texts: Rasmussen, Larry, *Earth Community, Earth Ethics* (Maryknoll, NY: Orbis Books, 1998); and Bouma-Prediger, Steven, *For the Beauty of the Earth: A Christian Vision for Creation Care* (Grand Rapids, MI: Baker, 2001). However, we also recommend the following for further exploration: Wilkinson, Loren (ed.), *Earthkeeping in the '90s: Stewardship of Creation* (Grand Rapids, MI: Eerdmans, 1991); DeWitt, Calvin B., *Earth Wise: A Biblical Response to Environmental Issues* (Grand Rapids, MI: CRC Publications, 1994); Van Dyke, Fred, et. al., *Redeeming Creation: The Biblical Basis for Environmental Stewardship* (Downers Grove, IL: InterVarsity Press, 1996); DeWitt, Calvin B., *Caring for Creation: Responsible Stewardship of God's Handiwork* (Grand Rapids, MI: Baker Books, 1998); Walsh, Brian, & Sylvia Keesmaat, *Colossians Remixed: Subverting the Empire* (Downers Grove, IL: InterVarsity Press, 2004).

26   Bouma-Prediger (2001), p. 135.

27   Rasmussen (1998) p. 76.

28   See especially Rasmussen (1998), pp. 282-294 and Bouma-Prediger (2001), pp. 105-110.

29   See Brueggemann, *Walter, The Land: Place as Gift, Promise, and Challenge in Biblical Faith* (Philadelphia: Augsburg Fortress, 1977); and also Wright, Christopher, *Old Testament Ethics for the People of God* (Downers Grove, IL: InterVarsity Press, 2004).

30   Rasmussen (1998) p. xii.

31   See Walsh, Brian, Marianne B. Karsh & Nik Ansell, "Trees, Forestry, and the Responsiveness of Creation," in *Cross Currents*, 44:2 (Summer 1994).

32   Bouma-Prediger (2001) p. 37.

33   Orr, David, *The Nature of Design: Ecology, Culture and Human Intention* (New York, Oxford Univ. Press, 2002) p. 209. See also Orr, David, *Ecological Literacy: Education and the Transition to a Postmodern World* (Albany, NY: SUNY Press, 1992) p. 4.

34   Orr, David, *Earth in Mind: On Education, Environment, and the Human Prospect* (Washington, DC: Island Press, 1994) p. 27.

35   Orr (1992) p. 84.

36   Orr (1994) p. 33.

37   Orr (1992) p. 133.

38   Orr (1992) p. 92.

39   Orr (1992) pp. 90-92. The other five foundations of an ecological educa- tion are these: (1) all education is environmental education in what it teaches (or doesn't) about our connection with the earth; (2) multiplicity and connectivity – holistic and interdisciplinary education; (3) prioritizing local, particular and specific places in order to avoid being too abstract; (4) pedagogy (process) is as important as curriculum (content); (5) enhanced competence with natural systems.

40   Orr (1992) p. 134.

41   Orr (1994) p. 52.

42   Orr (1994) p. 43.

43   Orr (1992) p. 92.

44   Orr (1994) p. 148.

45   Orr (2002) p. 201.

46   Orr (1992) p. 101.

47   Walsh & Keesmaat (2004).

48   Walsh (1992) p. 14.

49   Indeed, we suggest that the clearest examples of the subversive power of the gospel in both a pedagogical and teleological sense are narrated in the Scriptures. Christ himself was a master subversive storyteller in his use of parables. See Wright, N. T., *Jesus and the Victory of God* (Philadelphia: Augsburg Fortress, 1997) pp. 181-182.

50   CCSP is a member of the Christians for Environmental Stewardship (CES) Network and has an academic committee that oversees the program.

51   Each fall semester we also have a nursing track. Although these students take almost all the core courses, certain exceptions are made due to work- load.

52   For example, the question students invariably ask after traveling by boat to Calabash Caye for Marine Ecology is "Are you for real? This is education?" By the end of the course – lectures, discussions, reading, and eight or more snorkeling sessions – students are also well aware of the human threats to the reef from tourists, global warming, shrimp farming, soil ero-

sion, and so on. Each threat is a critique of the way our societies relate to nature and of the way we thoughtlessly consume, failing to consider the downstream consequences. The beauty of the reef therefore creates opportunities to facilitate a subversive critique of the political and economic status quo.

53   "Our" and "we" in the following discussions of fieldtrips are understood as including students, staff, and faculty. Certain literary license has been made in assuming that "we" moved through the experience together. Of course, education in general, and fieldtrips in particular, are never engaged with as singular experiences. Nevertheless, as a community "we" did share much of what happened here.

54   Emmons, Katherine M. et. al., *Cockscomb Basin Wildlife Sanctuary: Its History, Flora, and Fauna, for Visitors, Teachers, and Scientists* (Gay Mills, WI: Orang-utan Press, 1996).

55   Emmons et. al. (1996) pp. 14-17.

56   Kricher, John, *A Neotropical Companion: An Introduction to the Animals, Plants, and Ecosystems of the New World Tropics* (Princeton, NJ: Princeton Univ. Press, 1997).

57   This brief history is drawn from the following: Post, Thomas, "Legume Cover Cropping in Belize: Its Agronomic Potential and the Role of Farmer Experimentation in its Development" (Unpublished doctoral dissertation, School of Development Studies, University of East Anglia, Norwich, UK, 1998); Belize Sugar Industries Ltd., "A Short History of the Sugar Industry In Belize" (Unpublished promotional leaflet, Tower Hill, Belize, no date); and personal communication with Alfonso Vellejos.

58   The first boom took place in about 1878, with a significant bust in 1883 as a result of a dip in the UK market due to the introduction of the sugar beet. The next boom took place in the 1950s and early '60s as a result of preferential quotas instituted by the UK, improvements in processing facilities, and the opening of opportunities to small-scale farmers. However, a decline in the industry followed quickly (1967-1972) due to a downturn in global sugar prices. Another high took place in 1975, followed by another dip between 1982 and 1985. Prices have continued to be unstable since then.

59   The following are mentioned by our guide: increased competition from artificial sweeteners, an aggressive industrialized sugar industry in Australia, labor exploitation in Brazil, and the impending demise of preferential access of Belizean sugar to previously guaranteed markets in Europe and the United States.

60   Among those mentioned are poor diet causing diabetes, accidents related to the heavy equipment and hard labor associated with the sugar industry, chemical poisoning from papaya sprays.

61   The PUP and UDP are the two political parties in Belize. Loyalty to each party can be strong and consequently quite divisive in rural villages like Patchakan.

Bibliography

Anderson, Chris, *Teaching as Believing: Faith in the University* (Waco, TX: Baylor Univ. Press, 2004).

Belize Sugar Industries Ltd., "A Short History of the Sugar Industry In Belize" (Unpublished promotional leaflet, Tower Hill, Belize, no date).

Boff, Leonardo, "Salvation in Liberation: The Theological Meaning of Socio-historical Liberation" in Boff, Leonardo & Clodovis Boff, *Salvation and Liberation: In Search of a Balance Between Faith and Politics* (Maryknoll, NY: Orbis Books, 1979).

Bouma-Prediger, Steven, *For the Beauty of the Earth: A Christian Vision for Creation Care* (Grand Rapids, MI: Baker, 2001)

Bouma-Prediger, Steven, & Brian J. Walsh, "Education for Homelessness or Homemaking? The Christian College in a Postmodern Culture," in *Christian Scholars Review*, 32:3 (Spring 2003) pp. 281-295.

Brueggemann, Walter, *The Land: Place as Gift, Promise, and Challenge in Biblical Faith* (Philadelphia, Augsburg Fortress, 1977).

DeWitt, Calvin B., *Earth Wise: A Biblical Response to Environmental Issues* (Grand Rapids, MI: CRC Publications, 1994).

DeWitt, Calvin B., *Caring for Creation: Responsible Stewardship of God's Handiwork* (Grand Rapids, MI: Baker Books, 1998).

Emmons, Katherine M. et al., *Cockscomb Basin Wildlife Sanctuary: Its History, Flora, and Fauna, for Visitors, Teachers, and Scientists* (Gay Mills, WI: Orang-utan Press, 1996).

Kricher, John, *A Neotropical Companion: An Introduction to the Animals, Plants, and Ecosystems of the New World Tropics* (Princeton, NJ: Princeton Univ. Press, 1997).

Myers, Ched, *Binding the Strong Man: A Political Reading of Mark's Story of Jesus* (New York: Orbis Books, 1988).

Noll, Mark, *The Scandal of the Evangelical Mind* (Grand Rapids, MI: Eerdmans, 1995).

Orr, David, *Ecological Literacy: Education and the Transition to a Postmodern World* (Albany, NY: SUNY Press, 1992).

Orr, David, *Earth in Mind: On Education, Environment, and the Human Prospect* (Washington, DC: Island Press, 1994).

Orr, David, *The Nature of Design: Ecology, Culture and Human Intention* (New York, Oxford Univ. Press, 2002).

Post, Thomas, "Legume Cover Cropping in Belize: Its Agronomic Potential and the Role of Farmer Experimentation in its Development" (Unpublished doctoral dissertation, School of Development Studies, University of East Anglia, Norwich, UK, 1998).

Rasmussen, Larry, *Earth Community, Earth Ethics* (Maryknoll, NY: Orbis Books, 1998).

Rockell, Brenda "Ritual, Church and World: Building Up the Body of Christ, Connecting with the Culture Beyond the Church" (Unpublished manuscript, Auckland, New Zealand, 2005).

Van Dyke, Fred et al., *Redeeming Creation: The Biblical Basis for Environmental Stewardship* (Downers Grove, IL: InterVarsity, 1996).

Wallis, Jim, *God's Politics: Why the Right Gets It Wrong and the Left Doesn't Get It* (New York: HarperSanFrancisco, 2005).

Walsh, Brian, *Subversive Christianity: Imaging God in a Dangerous Time* (Seattle, WA: Alta Vista College Press, 1992).

Walsh, Brian, Marianne B. Karsh & Nik Ansell, "Trees, Forestry, and the Responsiveness of Creation," in *Cross Currents*, 44:2 (Summer 1994).

Walsh, Brian, & Sylvia Keesmaat, *Colossians Remixed: Subverting the Empire* (Downers Grove, IL: InterVarsity, 2004).

Wilkinson, Loren (ed.), *Earthkeeping in the '90s: Stewardship of Creation* (Grand Rapids, MI: Eerdmans, 1991).

Wolterstorff, Nicholas, *Educating for Life: Reflections on Christian Teaching and Learning*, ed. Gloria Goris Stronks & Clarence W. Joldersma (Grand Rapids, MI: Baker Academic, 2002).

Wolterstorff, Nicholas, *Educating for Shalom: Essays on Christian Higher Education*, ed. Clarence W. Joldersma & Gloria Goris Stronks (Grand Rapids, MI: Baker Academic, 2004).

Wolterstorff, Nicholas, *Until Justice and Peace Embrace* (Grand Rapids, MI: Eerdmans, 1983).

Wright, Christopher, *Old Testament Ethics for the People of God* (Downers Grove, InterVarsity Press, 2004).

Wright, N.T., *Jesus and the Victory of God* (Philadelphia: Augsburg Fortress, 1997).

Yoder, John Howard, *The Politics of Jesus* (Grand Rapids, MI: Eerdmans, 1972).

JE&CB 10:2 (2006) 91–110   1366-5456

Doug Blomberg

The Formation of Character: Spirituality Seeking Justice

EDUCATION ALWAYS DEPENDS on a view of humanness. Howard Gardner's influential theory of multiple intelligences promotes a broader view of human abilities than that generally favored in schooling, but Gardner relegates ethical, spiritual, and other normative dimensions to the periphery. The paper argues that virtue ethics, despite historical Protestant antipathy (which is addressed), provides a more comprehensive perspective, as long as the development of the virtues is seen to be embedded in creation and community. A biblical understanding of spirituality supplies the core that is missing from Gardner's bundle of computational competences, and seeking God's justice is its proper goal.

Schooling for What?

Mass schooling has traditionally favored verbal and logical-mathematical understandings. Despite efforts to draw a broader map of the pedagogical terrain, this orientation has intensified its hold on the territory of schooling over the past twenty years, as evidenced by an increasing emphasis on testing of literacy and numeracy skills and content acquisition. But, as Nel Noddings wrote recently in *Educational Leadership*,

> Surely, we should demand more from our schools than to educate people to be proficient in reading and mathematics. Too many highly proficient people commit fraud, pursue paths to success marked by greed, and care little about how their actions affect the lives of others.[1]

Elsewhere in the same issue, in a claim reminiscent of Paulo Freire, Elliot Eisner states that education is "a political undertaking because it reveals in its practice a conception of human nature, a view of the human mind, an image of what the young can become, and a vision that can guide us as we try to invent the future."[2] Werner Jaeger suggested that the Greeks were the first to recognize that education is a deliberate molding of human character in accordance with a community ideal.[3] A view of life's meaning and purpose is fundamentally spiritual and direction-setting, and it is unsurprising that opinions about the ideal differ, as Aristotle noted:

> There is no general agreement as to what young people should learn that is conducive either to [virtue] or to the best life; neither is it clear whether education should be more concerned with intellectual or moral character.... There is no agreement ... about the means to virtue, the various definitions of which have understandably led to different views about its practice.[4]

Plural Excellences?

Howard Gardner's theory of multiple intelligences may be considered an endeavor to resolve disputes between the various definitions of virtue by positing a plurality of human excellences. In one of the most influential contemporary attempts to redraw the map of cultural capital from which curricula derive, Gardner proposes that humans possess a range of distinct abilities or competences: linguistic, musical, logical-mathematical, spatial, bodily-kinesthetic, interpersonal, intrapersonal, and naturalist.[5] Designating these abilities "intelligences" was a deliberately provocative challenge to the concept of a single, general intelligence (g). Gardner claims that this is "a new definition of human nature," on a par with those offered by figures such as Socrates and Freud.[6] Having proffered this ideal, it is no surprise that Gardner adopts a prophetic tone when he claims that the great challenge we face in the new millennium is how best to realize our potential as "a species exhibiting several intelligences."[7]

However, Gardner regards the decision as to how to deploy the intelligences as a question of values, not one that can be settled by intelligence itself, which, as "computational power," is value-free. While affirming that both the intelligences and morality must be nurtured, he believes it "a grave error to confuse the two."[8] For him, our world is one in which the "division between the 'true' and the 'good' has been entrenched ... the fact that many other cultures meld the realms of knowledge and virtue leaves most contemporary Westerners untouched, if not bewildered."[9] He thus excludes spiritual and moral abilities from his array of intelligences, and only half-heartedly admits – or is it, half admits? – existential intelligence, as the most cognitive form of concern about "the nature of existence ... and spiritual or religious matters."[10] In a perhaps unintentional allusion to Plato's charioteer, Gardner recommends that the intelligences and morality, or normativity more generally, be yoked together as virtues.[11] But it remains problematic on his account as to how two such disparate realms could ever be equally yoked. While for Plato reason struggles to keep the soul and the appetites on an upward course, what holds the reins for Gardner?

Theodore Sizer, himself a significant figure in the field, says that "Gardner remains the premier American scholar addressing educational reform."[12] Certainly, many educators have adopted the theory of multiple intelligences with alacrity, and it has laudably boosted the recognition of individual differences, not only along one dimension but across several, thus supporting a horizontal rather than a vertical differentiation of students. Although Gardner is adamant that morality, character, emotional sensitivity, creativity, and wisdom are virtues that schools ought to sustain,[13] my concern is that the rhetoric in favor of these human qualities becomes submerged by the scientific and epistemological resources devoted to Gardner's "new definition of human nature." If the focus of schooling is on fostering multiple abilities and competences in respect to certain well-defined domains ("*knowing how*" and "*knowing that*"[14]), there is the real danger that nurturing dispositions to act normatively will take second place, if not be overlooked entirely. Gardner's theory focuses on "intellectual character" to the detriment of "moral character." The map of cultural capital needs to be more encompassing, whereas Gardner merely admits the lesser imperative that it be navigated with a moral compass. His broader intentions – noted earlier in this paragraph – would be better served if his insights into the richness of human functioning could be extricated from the dualistic methodology and anthropology in which they are currently embedded and incorporated in an integral perspective, in which spirituality and existential concerns are recognized as central rather than peripheral.

Virtues and Humanness

One starting point for such a reorientation, in accordance with Gardner's project of mapping human abilities and hinted at in his appeal to the integrative role of the virtues, may be found in recent discussions of "virtue ethics."[15] This was the dominant approach to ethical concerns until the modern era, when it was supplanted by efforts to find rule-based approaches to guide human action. In both its deontological and consequentialist forms, the modernist concern has been to articulate principles that will help the moral agent determine – "computationally," as it were – what is the one right thing to do in a particular situation. But situations prove hostile to this kind of specification, and generalizations lose their authority when confronted with individual cases. It is increasingly recognized that what is needed in place of theoretical prescriptions is a greater understanding of the factors that lead a person to make right judgments and wise decisions.[16] Virtue-based approaches to ethics and epistemology move away from the centrality of propositional understanding, rooted as this orientation is in a conception of humans as definitively rational beings, to a consideration of the broader range of normative properties of human agents, and hence to the significance of *character*.

I agree with Aristotle, Eisner, and Gardner: education requires a vision of what it means to be a *person*. Etymologically, "virtue" derives from the Latin *virtus*, with the root of *vir* ("man"). Virtue is "proper manliness," what it means to be truly a person. The remaining masculinist overtones (physical courage is linked to "virility," for instance) might well raise some matters for scrutiny, specifically in respect to whether virtue ethics is an ethics of self-sufficiency rather than one of relationality; feminists have, however, elaborated forms of virtue ethics that emphasize the relational dimension, in an "ethics of caring," for example.[17] From a biblical perspective, such a relational emphasis is crucial, as I will later elaborate.

Proper Humanness

Virtue can thus be construed as that which is constitutive of proper humanness, of the flourishing that is appropriate to us as the kind of beings we are. For Aristotle and his heirs, this consists in a life of reason: virtues are therefore attributes and manners of acting that are in accord with reason. Aristotle distinguished between two kinds of reasoning, one taking abstract universals as its subject matter, and the other, *phronesis* (practical reasoning or wisdom embedded in *praxis*), beginning with the intuition of value.[18] Deliberating on the steps required to actualize that value, we discern what is possible for us here and now, we decide for it, and then act.[19] It is as we habituate ourselves to acting in ways that are proper to our humanity that we acquire the virtues.

Martin Luther opposed any suggestion that people can make themselves worthy by their own effort or natural abilities. It is no hyperbole to say that he detested Aristotle, likening him to the devil incarnate, and regarding the notion that moral virtues can be acquired "the worst enemy of grace."[20] Reason may be applied to secular affairs, but it is useless when it comes to distinguishing ultimate human purposes or what is truly of *value*. The latter lies in the hands of God alone, as a gift of his grace.[21]

I can agree with Luther – but not quite as he framed the matter. The relation between the "spiritual" and the "secular" was for him paradoxical, effectively sequestering the rational from the spiritual-moral, and limiting the scope of both. His was a two-realm view of life, in which one's calling in the world – even when this was, for a ruler, for example, putatively in pursuit of justice – was unlikely to be compatible with one's calling as a Christian: "It is not impossible for a prince to be a Christian, although it is a rare thing and beset with many difficulties."[22]

While an abundant life is comprehensively spiritual, it is true that spirituality is in itself no guarantee in a fallen world of an abundant life. Spirituality is a matter of where one sets one's heart, on things above or things below (Col 3:1-2). While acknowledging duality, however, this is by no means to frame matters dualistically, in a counsel of world-flight, for Paul's concerns here are as down to earth as they can be.[23] It is rather an issue of life direction, either a commitment to God in Christ as the source of order and meaning or an investment in something created. If not a connection to the transcendent in spirit and truth, it is a fixation on the creaturely, and from this perspective, an obeisance to reason as the touchstone of the good life is itself an act of idolatry. But this does not require us to deny that adherence to the norms of rationality as one dimension of human functioning is essential to a life of flourishing.

Our understanding of education, politics, and much else besides, is directed by a vision of proper humanness. Gardner's proposal that "First-hand acquaintance with exemplary models probably constitutes the first step in becoming a person of multiple virtues" is an implicit acknowledgment of this.[24] Similarly, one of the features of virtue ethics is an emphasis on the importance of emulating models of virtue. In a Christian virtue ethics, Christ is to be our model, to whose image we are to be conformed more and more. The virtues are an expression of Christlikeness.[25] Though we can think of this in terms of the formation of character, we should also underscore that character is not a self-contained possession, but an ongoing life-direction, walking Christ-wise, we might say.[26] It is the spirit of one's life that matters, that it should be Holy Spirited: this is Paul's view of "good character" (e.g., Rom 8:1-17, 26-27).

If a virtue ethics is to be viable, we must recover an integral rather than a two-realm view of human life, whether the latter is construed in terms of nature and grace, theory and practice, or facts and values. Although the radical and comprehensive scope of Christ's redemptive life, death and resurrection has been obscured in many (if not all) Christian traditions, a perspective that is more faithful to Scripture will trust in the hope of substantial healing and the reconciliation of all things.[27] Then, a Christian virtue ethics is not an oxymoron. Growth to maturity, sanctification, can be conceived as the building of character and the practice of the virtues, not humans "bootstrapping," but working out their salvation in fear and trembling as God is at work in them (Phil 2:12-13).[28]

As we have seen, it is this integral perspective that eludes Gardner. Though the positivist era, in which "facts" and "values" were not only radically dichotomized, but all "values-talk" was construed as nonsensical,[29] has seemingly been succeeded by postmodernity, in which the ineradicability of communal and personal standpoints – and hence, of values – in knowing has been acknowledged, he can yet opine, "We probably will never re-create an Eden where intellectual and ethical values commingle, and we should recognize that these virtues can be separate. Indeed,… these virtues are often all too remote from one another."[30] There may be a hint of nostalgia in Gardner's observation; for Noddings, as we saw, this separation is a matter for outright lament.

Spirituality and Justice

My title suggests that character can be thought of in terms of life direction animated ("spirited") by the pursuit of justice. This betokens my conviction that the abundant, Spirit-filled life is one not of world flight but of world embrace. It is a life dedicated to the celebration – and, in a fallen world, restoration – of right relations between all things in Christ. When Jesus charges us to seek first and foremost God's kingdom and justice (Matt 6:33), to pray that God's kingdom should come to earth (Matt 6:10), to hunger and thirst for justice even though we may expect to be persecuted for our efforts (Matt 5:6, 10), he sets the pursuit of God's just rule at the core of human spirituality.[31]

In a similar vein, the doctrine of creation is more concerned with the ongoing relationship of God with creation in a covenantal order of justice than it is with origins.[32] In a recent article, Wendell Berry cites Psalm 104:30 and Job 34:14-15 as explicit statements of what elsewhere in Scripture he finds always implicit, "that all creatures live by participating in the life of God, by partaking of his Spirit and breathing his breath."[33] He explains further:

> When Jesus speaks of having life more abundantly, this, I think, is the life he means: a life that is not reducible by division, category or degree, but is one thing, heavenly and earthly, spiritual and material, divided only insofar as it is embodied in distinct creatures. He is talking about a finite world that is infinitely holy, a world of time that is filled with life that is eternal. His offer of more abundant life, then, is not an invitation to declare ourselves as certified "Christians," but rather to become conscious, consenting and responsible participants in the one great life….[34]

A life of true spirituality is one in pursuit of wholeness, healthiness: a life of holiness.[35] The injunction not to put asunder what God has joined is applicable to all the interrelationships we have within the web of creation. Contrary to all-too-common conceptions, spirituality is mundane (of this world), secular (of this age), and quotidian (everyday), being connected to all things, which have their coherence in Christ (Col 1:15-20). And where the joints have been severed by sin, our calling is to bring healing.[36] Spirituality and justice are two sides of one coin, for both are concerned with (restoring) right relations.[37]

Schooling for What?

Our opening question remains, however: is the building of character a legitimate aim for a school? Should not a school – as Noddings' and Eisner's antagonists propose – focus on academic goals, aiming at skill mastery and intellectual excellence, and leave the nurture of other sides of humanness to other institutions? Not only secular arguments in favor of "academic excellence," but also neo-Calvinist ones appealing to structural pluralism,[38] come into play. Here, a virtue perspective on *epistemology* suggests that what one knows is not so much a matter of what one is justified by reason(s) in believing as it is of what one *ought* to believe: there is no such thing as purely "calculative" or "computational" reasoning, for it is never outside a value context. It is, in Aristotelian terms for the moment, a species of practical reason, and is denatured when it is assumed to be detached from normativity. Thinking always proceeds in subjection to norms, both logical (on the side of the thinker) and non-logical (on the side of what is being thought about).

Human nature abhors a values vacuum. Where true spirituality is evicted, a host of pseudo-values rush in to take up residence. Reasoning becomes not value-free, but vicious. Nothing symbolizes better the depths to which so-called computational intelligence – intelligence construed as method – can sink than the Wannsee Conference in 1942, convened to map the contours of the "final solution." It should give us pause, as Gardner himself intimates,[39] to reflect that half of the participants possessed PhDs.

Reason Within the Bounds of Religion

The biblical picture of creation – which is all that there is, other than God – is that it is imbued with value, by the very fact that God chose to make it. But the recognition that it is sourced and sustained by the Word of the Creator frees us from the spiritual drive to find absolute value anywhere within creation itself. It liberates us both to respect the integrity of all that

God has made – "[b]ecause it is"[40] – and to recognize that value is *relative*, because embedded in the relational web between God and all creatures.

Gardner proposes that existential intelligence is the cognitive, intellectual component of the human propensity to address matters of ultimate concern that is also given an outlet in spirituality and religion.[41] Once intelligence has done its work, only then may spiritual, moral, and other values be brought into play. Biblically, however, it is spirituality that precedes rationality. As Wolterstorff has put it (appropriately turning one of Immanuel Kant's titles inside out), reason is within the bounds of religion.[42] It is thus only proper that the belief content of one's authentic commitment function as control over one's reasoning. Roy Clouser argues that religious beliefs will necessarily operate this way in theorizing, even when they remain unacknowledged.[43] This is the core of the biblical teaching concerning the fear of the Lord as the frame and source of wisdom: as Gerhard Von Rad comments, Israel considered "effective knowledge about God … the only thing that puts a man in a right relationship with the objects of his perception…. Wisdom stands and falls according to the right attitude of man to God."[44] Contrary to the Greek (and Gardnerian) conception, character as spiritual direction prepares the way for knowledge.

Learning is about what one *ought* to believe, but rightly discerning the norms that obtain in and for creation depends on where one stands. For Paul, this is "in Christ," for only thus can thoughts be taken captive to the sovereign Lord (2 Cor 10:5). The effect of this is reflexive: a person's character – intellectual as much as moral character – is transformed, as minds are renewed in spiritual acts of worship. To cite Wolterstorff yet again, this is a matter of "tendency learning," which we might paraphrase as the development of dispositions to act in normative ways.[45]

In an important respect, this turns classical virtue ethics, with its traces of the Homeric, self-sufficient "man of courage," on its head – or at least, situates character more definitely in a creational, communal context, whereas for Aristotle, the life of flourishing consists in theoretical contemplation, an activity best pursued in isolation. His "great-souled man" is far from *magnanimous* in our contemporary understanding of this term, and Luther was certainly correct to be suspicious of Aristotle's proudly independent *megalopsychos*.[46] As Terry Eagleton observes, though Aristotle affirms the importance of the *polis*, virtue is for him only minimally a reciprocal matter, and "he does not really recognize that virtue is what happens between people – that it is a function of relationships."[47] It is significant that "soul" in Hebrew (*nepeš*) connotes the neediness, vulnerability, and dependence of the whole person as *image* of God; this is not the non-mortal, immaterial *substance* of the Greek *psychē*.[48]

A value-laden creation is prior to and evocative of virtuous character; as Paddy Walsh says, it is a condition of us having values that there is value to which we respond.[49] It is in relation to the God-given normativity of creation, including people and societal structures, that the virtues are formed. A virtuous person is not an isolate, a modern "individual *qua* individual,"[50] but can only be such as a responsible member of a community which has been shaped in "justice and equity" by his or her forebears.[51] According to Brian Walsh and Sylvia Keesmaat, the Apostle Paul teaches that Christians live as they do "because of the matrix of relationships that characterize new life in Christ, and especially because of a living relationship with the living Christ...."[52]

Subjective Realization of Value(s)

Despite a general Christian wariness of the subjectivism of values-talk, I wish to affirm the *necessarily* (though certainly not *exhaustively*) subjective nature of the virtues, for values are not accessible as absolutes beyond experience but only as they are realized within a cultural horizon. This form of non-radical constructivism reminds us that in developing virtue we are *subjecting* ourselves to the law of God, which is love. The responsive nature of the virtues should then satisfy Luther that there is no "works righteousness" involved in a properly Christian virtue ethics. The pluriform values of creation (and here, Augustine was right in his assimilation of the classical virtues to love, for all may be regarded as responses to the Great Commandments) constitute the law to which normative human responses are subject. Creational normativity – the truth God speaks in and through creation – in-*forms* and en-*courages* us, calls us to have the courage that is necessary to live virtuously in a fallen world; and when God calls, God also empowers.[53]

A person of character acts justly and with integrity. The book of Proverbs makes clear that "the getting of wisdom" requires instruction in righteousness, justice, and equity (1:3), and exemplifies that the forming of godly traits is not an idle ambition. The "getting of wisdom" is as good a way as any of framing a biblical goal of learning, and it is a holy, holistic one.

Wisdom may be construed as the "realization of value," in the two senses of realization, as *understanding* and *actualizing*.[54] But "understanding" in this definition ought not to be overly intellectualized: it is *standing under*, subjecting oneself to revealed value. When MacIntyre suggests that the virtues consist in the kind of responsiveness that enables one to "recognize in one's practice what goods are at stake in this or that particular situation and what the threats to them are and to find in those goods premises for an argument whose conclusion will be a just action,"[55] he captures the situated normativity that is important to wisdom,[56] and intimates the ubiquity of justice as a criterion for action, but places it within an Aristotelian frame. Yes, the goods can be re-cognized, but only if we have a broader notion of cognition than one that identifies it with reason and the intellect, and sets it over against affect and conation.

Cognition is a whole-person activity. *The realization of value*, not the likening of the structure of human action to an argument, is a preferable description, because "realization" allows of a pluralistic interpretation: good thinking is the realization of logical value, good painting of aesthetic value, stewardship of economic value – and so on, for language, morality, and justice. It is not reasoning that is central in our pursuit of the varying goods, but the spirit that influences us. This perspective transcends and at the same time subsumes the dichotomizing of reason into the pure and the practical in recognition of a diversity of "ways of wisdom," the requirement for a simultaneous realization of a plurality of values.[57] Gardner has certainly caught the scent of the many-sidedness of human functioning, and implicitly acknowledges the need for simultaneous realization when he identifies exemplary persons as those who combine in their actions a range of virtues, "who have musical *and* interpersonal intelligence, who are psychometrically intelligent *and* creative in the arts, who combine emotional sensitivity *and* a high standard of moral conduct."[58] Similarly, he suggests that "a person who can use several intelligences together appropriately is more likely to be wise."[59] But the integral unity of personhood will necessarily escape a description in terms of a bundle of characteristics or the melding of disparate realms of "fact" and "value."

Character: A Characteristic Way of Going

None of these just-listed attainments comes easily in a fallen creation that is at the same time dynamically structured by the Word of God, and historically and culturally complex because given into the care of humankind to till and tend to God's glory. The realization of value is as often as not problematic, to say the least, as the Cross of Christ most poignantly attests. Justice is not readily won. The discrepancy between what is – current, value-laden, vice-ridden facticity – and what ought to be, presents us with constant challenges to be addressed. But the pervasiveness of sin is the best justification for education of the whole person, the formation of *character*, for there is no area of life that is spiritually neutral, and the cosmic scope of Christ's work of redemption is the only basis for hope that it is a goal there is point in pursuing.

A formative emphasis on growth rather than on universal standards of achievement assessed summatively comports well with a Christian eschatological perspective, in its recognition of the "now but not yet" quality of life. Perfection is not a state that may be attained here and now. Yet God expects a movement toward maturity, and because God calls us, it is possible. Our new selves are being continuously renewed (Col 3:10). Problems – the ultimate ones of injustice, suffering and death – cannot be obliterated. It is not the solution or avoidance of problems that is promised, but the strength and courage to deal with them in faith, hope and above all, love (1 Cor 13:13). Paul goes so far as to claim that we may rejoice in our sufferings, because suffering produces perseverance, which leads in turn to character, which is a life of hope, looking beyond the present in the expectation of the future, drawn forward by the Spirit of God (Rom 5:1-5).

William Brown suggests *formation, deformation,* and *reformation* of character as a key to understanding the biblical Wisdom Literature,[60] in which a life of character is not one of "rule following," because living requires an openness and vulnerability to slings and arrows, an ability to persevere, as the New Testament's preeminent wisdom writer affirms (Jas 1:2-4). Rules, of the kind favored by modernist approaches to ethics, may establish constraints, but they cannot dictate action that is truly sensitive to the moment and to the norms inviting realization in it. A person of character is a person of integrity, who responds faithfully to the norms for human living. Such persons come to know the right thing to do, and are disposed to do it, because they entreat God whole-heartedly for wisdom (Jas 1:5-8). Luther called James's letter an "epistle of straw" because it seemed to him to embody the very attitude he so despised in Aristotle. But James's assertion of human responsibility shares Paul's confidence that "the just shall live by faith" (Rom 1:17, Gal 3:11), emphasizing, however, that faith leads to living a just life.

God's world – in which we hear God's voice – cries out for the instantiation of value, inviting responses-in-action. In these ongoing responsive encounters, we hope that normative action develops over time into a disposition in our students (as in ourselves) to act normatively. It is freely chosen purposeful response to problems posed, directed by and toward normative ends, which I take be suggestive of the rhythm of learning.[61]

Conclusion

I commenced this paper by illustrating the importance of a view of humanness to an understanding of the purposes of education and suggesting that, while Gardner's "new conception of human nature" makes a significant contribution by elaborating some of the rich complexity of being human beyond the narrowly rational, it threatens to burden pedagogy with a sorely misplaced focus. As pluralistic as the theory is, it relegates normative human abilities – the domain explored by virtue ethics – to the periphery. And Gardner's "multiply intelligent" person is a bundle of computational competences without a "heart." While applauding his earnest desire that intelligences and values be yoked together as virtues, a more integral conception is required for such a union to succeed – indeed, a conception that identifies a prior unity. It is the whole person who acts – which is why Gardner can claim emulation of admirable people as the pedagogical route to becoming a multiply virtuous person.[62]

I have proposed that a Christian virtue perspective, honoring the creational, communal context in which the virtues develop, supports a conception of educational purposes as the formation of character or the getting of wisdom, the "multiple intelligences" finding a place within this more comprehensive frame. And far from being a peripheral human trait, I have affirmed the biblical view that spirituality goes "all the way down," to our fundamental choices concerning whom or what we will serve (1 Ki 18:21). Prevaricate as we do in this commitment, it is this that defines who we are, and which *inspires* our deployment of whatever "intelligences" we have.

If the "wizardry" of the *Harry Potter* series indeed incorporates some wisdom, then it might lie in the words of his Hogwarts headmaster, Albus Dumbledore: "It is our choices, Harry, that show what we truly are, far more than our abilities."[63] The great challenge of this (or any) millennium is not that of realizing our intelligences but choosing a life-direction of "right-wise-ness" toward God's justice coming, in which all the normative dimensions of humanness are realized. Justice is a primary spiritual value, because God wills that all creatures be respected in the integrity with which they have been made. The ways of wisdom are paths of peace (Prov 3:17), but this *shalom* is not mere absence of conflict; it is the vibrant and dynamic mutual responsiveness that is the expression of a just order. Because the full flourishing of persons consists in their standing in right relationships with God and all that God has made, the formation of virtuous character requires spirituality that seeks after justice.

Notes

1   Noddings, Nel, "What Does It Mean to Educate the Whole Child?" in
    Educational Leadership, 63:1 (September 2005) p. 8. The theme of this
    issue is "The whole child," and it carries articles on social justice, multicul-
    turalism, nutrition and exercise, multi-age grouping and character educa-
    tion, with passing references to spirituality.

2   Eisner, Elliot W., "Back to Whole" in *Educational Leadership*, 63:1
    (September 2005) p. 18.

3   Jaeger, Werner, *Paideia: The Ideals of Greek Culture*, 2nd ed., trans.
    Gilbert Highet (New York: Oxford Univ. Press, 1945) pp. xii, xiv.

4   Aristotle, *Politics*, trans. and ed. John Warrington (London: J. M. Dent &
    Sons, 1959) pp. 221-222. The substitution of "virtue" (for "simple good-
    ness") in the second line follows *The Politics of Aristotle*, trans. T. A.
    Sinclair (Harmondsworth, UK: Penguin, 1962), VIII:1.

5   The first extended exposition of the theory is in Gardner, Howard, *Frames
    of Mind: The Theory of Multiple Intelligences* (New York: Basic Books,
    1983). The "naturalist intelligence" was a later addition, as described in
    Gardner, Howard, *Intelligence Reframed: Multiple Intelligences for the
    21st Century* (New York: Basic Books, 1999) pp. 47-52.

6   Gardner (1999) p. 44. Though Gardner qualifies this statement with the
    phrase, "cognitively speaking," it is nonetheless "an account of human
    cognition in its fullness...." When favored definitions of humanness
    include "rational animal" and "*homo sapiens*," this may not be much of a
    limitation at all.

7   Gardner (1999) p. 45.

8   Gardner (1999) p. 46, cf. p. 4.

9   Gardner (1999) p. 68.

10 Gardner (1999) p. 60.

11 Gardner (1999) p. 46.

12 Sizer is quoted on the back cover of Gardner (1999).

13 For example, Gardner (1999) pp. 132-134, 210-212.

14 Gardner (1999) p. 55.

15 For discussions directly relevant to education, see, for example, Carr, David
    & Jan Steutel (eds.), *Virtue Ethics and Moral Education* (New York:
    Routledge, 1999); Higgins, Christopher, "MacIntyre's Moral Theory and the
    Possibility of an Aretaic Ethics of teaching" in *Journal of Philosophy of
    Education* 37:2 (2003) pp. 279-292. (Virtue ethics is also termed "aretaic
    ethics," from the Greek equivalent of *virtus*, *arētē*.) David Gill's *Becoming
    Good: Building Moral Character* (Downers Grove, IL: InterVarsity Press,
    2000) elaborates an evangelical virtue ethics. Acknowledging its roots in
    Classical Greek philosophy, Gill notes that Augustine and Aquinas both
    adopted this approach, and specifically the four cardinal virtues of justice,

wisdom, courage, and temperance or self-control. Augustine incorporated these within the framework of Paul's "theological virtues" of faith, hope and love, seeing the classical virtues as four forms of love. Aquinas regarded them as "natural" virtues, helping us to achieve our natural end of happiness; he supplemented them with the three "supernatural virtues," which are necessary if we are to know God. As well as affirming the cardinal virtues as embedded in the New Testament, and offering a more integral perspective that is in this respect Augustinian rather than Thomistic, Gill's distinctive contribution is to add to the three Pauline virtues the further biblical virtue of holiness and the eight beatitudes. Noting that character is often related to the roles that we play – as parent, faculty member, citizen, for example – he groups this list of virtues around five roles the New Testament portrays, namely, disciple, servant, leader, peacemaker, and ambassador.

16   As an example of this recognition, Jim Garrison may be quoted: "Moral perception is a necessary part of the logic of practical reasoning. Practical reasoning is always contextual…. It deals with difficulties of doing the right thing in the right way and at the right time in response to problems posed by particular people, in particular places, on particular occasions. Moral perception is an indispensable part of practical reasoning because such perception is necessary for grasping the uniqueness of a practical context and the particularity of those participating in it. "Eventually we must rely on our perceptions to recognize that something, someone, or some situation is an instance of a given rule" (Garrison, Jim, *Dewey and Eros: Wisdom and Desire in the Art of Teaching* [New York and London: Teachers College Press, 1997] pp. 71-72).

17   Noddings, Nel, *Caring: A Feminine Approach to Ethics and Moral Education* (Berkeley and Los Angeles: Univ. of California Press, 1984); Noddings, Nel, *The Challenge to Care in Schools: An Alternative Approach to Education* (New York: Teachers College Press, 1992).

18   The ultimate value was that of the "good life" – *eudaimonia*: instructively, in the present context, having a "good spirit."

19   Garrison (1997) pp. xvii-ixx; MacIntyre, Alisdair, *After Virtue: A Study in Moral Theory*, 2nd ed. (Notre Dame, IN: Univ. of Notre Dame Press, 1984) pp. 161-162.

20   Painter, Mark, *The Depravity of Wisdom: The Protestant Reformation and the Disengagement of Knowledge from Virtue in Modern Philosophy* (Aldershot, UK: Ashgate Publishing Co., 1999) p. 73.

21   Painter (1999) pp. 71-76.

22   Luther, Martin, "Temporal Authority: To what Extent should it be Obeyed?" in Brandt, W. I. (ed.), *Luther's Works* (Philadelphia: Muhlenberg Press, 1962) p. 118.

23 See Walsh, Brian & Sylvia Keesmaat, *Colossians Remixed: Subverting the Empire* (Downers Grove, IL: InterVarsity Press, 2004) pp. 151-156.

24 Gardner (1999) pp. 210-211. Here he instances the intelligences, creativity, and morality as examples of the virtues.

25 We may recall that in Thomas Carlyle's translation of Luther's "Ein' Feste Burg," Jesus is the "proper man"; he is *rechte* – right(eous) and just.

26 This is not an idiosyncratic coining. "Righteousness" was originally "right-wise-ness," which may be construed as "a stable quality of a right way of going," and this usage is retained in forms such as "lengthwise" and "clockwise." See Potter, Simeon, *Our Language* (Harmondsworth, UK: Penguin, 1961) p. 37. This is also of interest in light of the theme of wisdom that will emerge below.

27 While John Calvin shared Luther's understanding of total depravity, and agreed that whatever goods humans attained, whether in their fallen or redeemed state, were gifts of God, he differed markedly from him in affirming that in Christ, humans are restored to their former glory, in knowledge (light of intellect), true righteousness (rectitude of heart) and holiness (soundness of every part). Calvin, John, *Institutes of the Christian Religion*, 2 vols., trans. Henry Beveridge (Grand Rapids, MI: Eerdmans, 1970) vol. I: XV, 4.

28 As the focus of this paper is on spirituality and justice, there is limited scope to explore the content of a Christian virtue ethics beyond these considerations. *Arētē* appears rarely in the New Testament (Phil 4:8; 1 Pet 2:9; 2 Pet 1:3, 5), and "virtues" only once in the NIV (Col 3:12-14), as an insertion by the translators. Nonetheless, the list of "virtues" Paul gives there is instructive: compassion, kindness, humility, gentleness, patience, forbearance, and forgiveness – and binding them together, love. For Machiavelli and Nietzsche, this is the ethics of the weak or the enslaved. For the Christian, it is the ethics of those who would willingly lay down their lives for their friends – and their enemies.

29 Cf. Ayer, A. J., *Language, Truth and Logic* (Harmondsworth, Middlesex: Penguin Books, 1971).

30 Gardner (1999) p. 211.

31 Nicholas Wolterstorff, in his keynote address to the Spirituality, Justice, and Pedagogy Conference (Calvin College, 2005), illustrated how translators' decisions to most often render *dikaiosunē* as "righteousness" rather than "justice" leads to a privatizing – what one might call (if one acknowledges a counterfeit notion of spirituality embedded in the term) a "spiritualizing" – of biblical faith. If we further recognize that "right" and "just" entered the English language as virtual *synonyms*, from Germanic (cf. note 25) and Romance sources respectively, the just actions of the Good Samaritan will more readily be seen to equate to righteousness. The parable addresses

the issue of who one's neighbor is and what it means to love one's neighbor as oneself (as one reviewer of this article noted), and Jesus makes plain that this does not consist in self-contained moral uprightness but in actions of care and compassion toward others.

32   Goldsworthy, Graeme, *Gospel and Wisdom: Israel's Wisdom Literature in the Christian Life* (Exeter, Devon & Flemington Markets, NSW: Paternoster Press & Lancer Books, 1987) pp. 132-138.

33   Berry, Wendell, "The Burden of the Gospels: An Unconfident Reader" in *Christian Century* (2005), http://www.christiancentury.org/article.lasso?id =1298 (21 November 2005).

34   Berry (2005), "The Burden of the Gospels."

35   The words *hale, whole, holy, healthy*, and *heal* all have their root in the Indo-European *kailo*. (*The American Heritage Dictionary of the English Language*, 4th ed. [Houghton Mifflin Co., 2000], http://www.bartleby.com/61/roots/IE198.html).

36   Spirituality as true religion then is also a re-binding (Lat. *re-ligare*) of ourselves to other creatures and to God. While Jacques Derrida acknowledges the limitations of etymology in determining the current meaning of a word, he suggests that the competing putative derivations of "religion" both concern "a persistent bond that bonds itself," although he emphasizes, "first and foremost to itself." Derrida, Jacques, "Faith and Knowledge: The Two Sources of 'Religion' at the Limits of Reason Alone" in Derrida, J. & G. Vattimo (eds.), *Religion* (Stanford, CA: Stanford Press, 1998) p. 37.

37   Wolterstorff also underscored the link between spirituality and justice I am here affirming in the keynote address cited above. He distinguished "primary justice" from what he argued was the more common Christian equation of justice with retribution.

38   These would be to the effect that schools have an academic calling, families have a more encompassing nurturing role, churches oversee the development of faith life, etc.

39   Gardner (1999) p. 205.

40   See Zuidervaart's comments on these three words, as they appear near the end of Margaret Atwood's *Oryx and Crake*. Zuidervaart, Lambert, *Artistic Truth: Aesthetics, Discourse, and Imaginative Disclosure* (Cambridge, UK: Cambridge Univ. Press, 2004) p. 371.

41   Gardner (1999) pp. 60, 76.

42   Wolterstorff, Nicholas, *Reason Within the Bounds of Religion* (Grand Rapids, MI: Eerdmans, 1976).

43   Clouser, Roy A., *The Myth of Religious Neutrality: An Essay on the Hidden Role of Religious Belief in Theories* (Notre Dame, IN, and London, UK: Univ. of Notre Dame Press, 1991).

44   Von Rad, Gerhard, *Wisdom in Israel*, trans. James D. Martin (London: SCM Press, 1972) pp. 67, 69.

45   Wolterstorff, Nicholas, *Educating for Responsible Action* (Grand Rapids, MI: CSI Publications/Eerdmans, 1980). Aristotle classifies virtues as dispositions (Aristotle [1953] II); Dewey is persuaded that beliefs are fundamentally dispositions to act (see Garrison [1997] p. 91).

46   Aristotle (1953) IV:3. MacIntyre (1999) comments that the "virtues of receiving" are "bound to be lacking in those whose forgetfulness of their dependence is expressed in an unwillingness to remember benefits conferred by others. One outstanding example, even perhaps *the* outstanding example of this type of bad character and also of a failure to recognize its badness is Aristotle's *megalopsychos*..." (p. 127).

47   Eagleton, Terry, *After Theory* (London, UK: Penguin, 2003) p. 168.

48   See note 28. Cf. Wolff, Hans Walter, *Anthropology of the Old Testament*, trans. Margaret Kohl (London: SCM Press, 1974) pp. 10-25.

49   Walsh, Paddy, *Education and Meaning: Philosophy in Practice* (London: Cassell Educational, 1993) p. 113.

50   MacIntyre, Alasdair, "Practical Rationalities as Forms of Social Structure" in Knight, Kelvin (ed.), *The MacIntyre Reader* (Notre Dame, IN: Univ. of Notre Dame Press, 1998) pp. 129-130.

51   Brown, William, *Character in Crisis: A Fresh Approach to the Wisdom Literature of the Old Testament* (Grand Rapids, MI, and Cambridge, UK: Eerdmans, 1996), p. 34; as the title of the book intimates, Brown's comment pertains to the covenant community of Israel. One reviewer of the present paper noted, however, that conventional understandings of "traits," "virtues," and "integrity" draw attention "away from systemic (in)justice to individual character," despite my attempt at re-framing. Given the emphasis on the importance of community in the learning of virtues, s/he asked, how it is possible to be just in an unjust society? "How would the project of reforming an unjust society get started if being virtuous both presupposes and must precede its realization?" The beginning of an answer is found in the next sentence of the article: the body of Christ is enabled by his power to start something truly new. Paul affirms that, while we are "hard pressed on every side ... perplexed ... persecuted" (for justice's sake? 2 Cor 4:8-9), in Christ there is "a new creation." We are given "the ministry of reconciliation," God having made Christ "to be sin for us, so that in him we might become the [justice] of God" (2 Cor 5:17-18, 21 NIV). The penultimate section of the paper further acknowledges the real difficulties of living faithfully in a fallen world.

52   Walsh & Keesmaat (2004) p. 156.

53   Although evidence for this might most readily be found in the Wisdom Literature (see Blomberg, Doug, "The Practice of Wisdom: Knowing

When" in *Journal of Education & Christian Belief*, 2:1 [1998] pp. 7-26), a couple of examples from Isaiah are instructive: God instructs farmers in the virtues of their vocation (28:23-29) – through wisdom accumulated and passed on by the farming community, one may assume – and assures us that God's word accomplishes the purposes for which it is spoken (55:9-13).

54   Maxwell, Nicholas, *From Knowledge to Wisdom: A Revolution in the Aims and Methods of Science* (Oxford: Basil Blackwell, 1984).

55   MacIntyre, Alasdair, *Dependent Rational Animals: Why Human Beings Need the Virtues* (Chicago and La Salle, IL: Open Court, 1999) p. 92.

56   See Blomberg (1998).

57   See Blomberg, Doug, "Ways of Wisdom: Multiple Modes of Meaning in Pedagogy and Andragogy" in Kok, John (ed.), *Ways of Knowing, in Concert* (Sioux Center, IA: Dordt College Press, 2005) pp. 123-146; cf. Goudzwaard, Bob, *Capitalism and Progress: A Diagnosis of Western Society*, trans. Josina Zylstra (Toronto, ON, and Grand Rapids, MI: Wedge/Eerdmans, 1979) p. 65.

58   Gardner (1999) pp. 210-211.

59   Gardner (1999) p. 133.

60   Brown (1996).

61   See Stronks, Gloria Goris & Doug Blomberg (eds.), *A Vision with a Task: Christian Schooling for Responsive Discipleship* (Grand Rapids, MI: Baker Book House, 1993), chapter 8, for an explication of a curricular model of play, problem-posing, and purposeful response. There is a resonance between this emphasis on "freely chosen purposeful response" – accentuated in the book's subtitle – and Aristotle's definition of virtue in terms of "purposive disposition," emphasizing actions that are done not mechanically or habitually but by active choice (Aristotle [1953] II, III). See also Blomberg, Doug, "A Problem-posing Pedagogy: 'Paths of Pleasantness and Peace'" in *Journal of Education & Christian Belief*, 3:2 (2000) pp. 97-113.

62   Lest the reader think I have put these last few words in Gardner's mouth, see the text referenced in note 24.

63   Cited in Grossman, Lev, "The Story So Far, Book by Book" in *TIME Canadian Edition* (23 June 2003) p. 54.

Bibliography

The American Heritage Dictionary of the English Language, 4th ed. (Houghton Mifflin Co., 2000), http://www.bartleby.com/61/roots/E198.html.

Aristotle, *The Ethics of Aristotle*, trans. J. A. K. Thomson (New York: Penguin, 1953).

Aristotle, *Politics*, trans. and ed. John Warrington (London: J. M. Dent & Sons, 1959).

Aristotle, *The Politics of Aristotle*, trans. T. A. Sinclair (Harmondsworth, UK: Penguin, 1962).

Ayer, A. J., *Language, Truth and Logic* (Harmondsworth, Middlesex: Penguin Books, 1971).

Berry, Wendell, "The Burden of the Gospels: An Unconfident Reader" in *Christian Century* (2005) http://www.christiancentury.org/article.lasso?id=1298 (21 November 2005).

Blomberg, Doug, "The Practice of Wisdom: Knowing When" in *Journal of Education & Christian Belief*, 2:1 (1998) pp. 7-26.

Blomberg, Doug, "A Problem-posing Pedagogy: 'Paths of Pleasantness and Peace'" in *Journal of Education & Christian Belief*, 3:2 (1999) pp. 97-113.

Blomberg, Doug, "Ways of Wisdom: Multiple Modes of Meaning in Pedagogy and Andragogy" in Kok, John (ed.), *Ways of Knowing, in Concert* (Sioux Center, IA: Dordt College Press, 2005) pp. 123-146.

Brown, William, *Character in Crisis: A Fresh Approach to the Wisdom Literature of the Old Testament* (Grand Rapids, MI, and Cambridge, UK: Eerdmans, 1996.)

Calvin, John, *Institutes of the Christian Religion*, 2 vols., trans. Henry Beveridge (Grand Rapids, MI: Eerdmans, 1970).

Carr, David & Jan Steutel (eds.), *Virtue Ethics and Moral Education* (New York: Routledge, 1999).

Clouser, Roy A., *The Myth of Religious Neutrality: An Essay on the Hidden Role of Religious Belief in Theories* (Notre Dame, IN, and London: Univ. of Notre Dame Press, 1991).

Derrida, Jacques, "Faith and Knowledge: The Two Sources of 'Religion' at the Limits of Reason Alone" in Derrida, J. & G. Vattimo (eds.), *Religion* (Stanford, CA: Stanford Press, 1998) pp. 1-78.

Eagleton, Terry, *After Theory* (London, UK: Penguin, 2003).

Eisner, Elliot W., "Back to Whole" in *Educational Leadership*, 63:1 (September 2005) pp. 14-18.

Gardner, Howard, *Frames of Mind: The Theory of Multiple Intelligences* (New York: Basic Books, 1983).

Gardner, Howard, *Intelligence Reframed: Multiple Intelligences for the 21st Century* (New York: Basic Books, 1999).

Garrison, Jim, *Dewey and Eros: Wisdom and Desire in the Art of Teaching* (New York and London: Teachers College Press, 1997).

Gill, David, *Becoming Good: Building Moral Character* (Downers Grove, IL: InterVarsity Press, 2000).

Goldsworthy, Graeme, *Gospel and Wisdom: Israel's Wisdom Literature in the Christian Life* (Exeter, Devon & Flemington Markets, NSW: Paternoster Press & Lancer Books, 1987).

Goudzwaard, Bob, *Capitalism and Progress: A Diagnosis of Western Society*, trans. Josina Zylstra (Toronto, ON, and Grand Rapids, MI: Wedge/Eerdmans, 1979).

Grossman, Lev, "The Story So Far, Book by Book" in *TIME Canadian Edition* (23 June 2003) pp. 54-55.

Higgins, Christopher, "MacIntyre's Moral Theory and the Possibility of an Aretaic Ethics of Teaching" in *Journal of Philosophy of Education*, 37:2 (2003) pp. 279-292.

Jaeger, Werner, *Paideia: The Ideals of Greek Culture*, 2nd ed., trans Gilbert Highet (New York: Oxford Univ. Press, 1945).

Knight, Kelvin (ed.), *The Macintyre Reader* (Notre Dame, IN: Univ. of Notre Dame Press, 1998).

Luther, Martin, "Temporal Authority: To what Extent should it be Obeyed?" in Brandt, W. I. (ed.), *Luther's Works* (Philadelphia: Muhlenberg Press, 1962).

MacIntyre, Alasdair, *Dependent Rational Animals: Why Human Beings Need the Virtues* (Chicago and La Salle, IL: Open Court, 1999).

MacIntyre, Alasdair, *After Virtue: A Study in Moral Theory*, 2nd ed. (Notre Dame, IN: Univ. of Notre Dame Press, 1984).

MacIntyre, Alasdair, "Practical Rationalities as Forms of Social Structure" in Knight, Kelvin (ed.), *The Macintyre Reader* (Notre Dame, IN: Univ. of Notre Dame Press, 1998) pp. 120-135.

Maxwell, Nicholas, *From Knowledge to Wisdom: A Revolution in the Aims and Methods of Science* (Oxford: Basil Blackwell, 1984).

Noddings, Nel, *Caring: A Feminine Approach to Ethics and Moral Education* (Berkeley and Los Angeles: Univ. of California Press, 1984).

Noddings, Nel, *The Challenge to Care in Schools: An Alternative Approach to Education* (New York: Teachers College Press, 1992).

Noddings, Nel, "What Does It Mean to Educate the Whole Child?" in *Educational Leadership*, 63:1 (September 2005) pp. 8-13.

Painter, Mark, *The Depravity of Wisdom: The Protestant Reformation and the Disengagement of Knowledge from Virtue in Modern Philosophy* (Aldershot, UK: Ashgate Publishing Co., 1999).

Potter, Simeon, *Our Language* (Harmondsworth, UK: Penguin, 1961).

Stronks, Gloria Goris & Doug Blomberg (eds.), *A Vision with a Task: Christian Schooling for Responsive Discipleship* (Grand Rapids, MI: Baker Book House, 1993).

Von Rad, Gerhard, *Wisdom in Israel*, trans. James D. Martin (London: SCM Press, 1972).

Walsh, Brian & Sylvia Keesmaat, *Colossians Remixed: Subverting the Empire* (Downers Grove, IL: InterVarsity Press, 2004).

Walsh, Paddy, *Education and Meaning: Philosophy in Practice* (London: Cassell Educational, 1993).

Wolff, Hans Walter, *Anthropology of the Old Testament*, trans. Margaret Kohl (London: SCM Press, 1974).

Wolterstorff, Nicholas, *Educating for Responsible Action* (Grand Rapids, MI: CSI Publications/Eerdmans, 1980).

Wolterstorff, Nicholas, *Reason Within the Bounds of Religion* (Grand Rapids, MI: Eerdmans, 1976).

Zuidervaart, Lambert, *Artistic Truth: Aesthetics, Discourse, and Imaginative Disclosure* (Cambridge, UK: Cambridge Univ. Press, 2004).

JE&CB 10:2 (2006) 111–128   1366-5456

Steven H. VanderLeest

Teaching Justice by Emphasizing the Non-neutrality of Technology

THIS CHAPTER EXPLORES the connection between justice and technology and its implications for teaching about technology and teaching technological design. The non-neutrality of technology in relation to issues of justice is examined, and pedagogical strategies are described for making students aware of this non-neutrality and enabling them to incorporate a concern for justice into their design decisions.

Introduction

What does technology have to do with justice? Technology is a product of engineers, the result of creative design, a tool for producing a particular end. Justice is a principle, an ideal, a societal norm. Can we learn anything about justice by examining technology? I believe so. In this paper I hope to demonstrate the relationship between justice and technology and simultaneously to explore methods of teaching this relationship. My interest in the subject stems from my position as a teacher and practitioner of engineering, the profession responsible for producing technology. I hope to teach my students that engineers are responsible not merely in the narrow sense of being the designers of technology, but in the broader sense of having moral responsibility for their creations. Engineering is an interdisciplinary profession that combines creativity, design, science, math, psychology, sociology, art, history, invention, and more to solve problems using technology. But this paper is not only for teachers of technology and engineering; it is also for those who teach users of technology, because justice concerns all those associated with technology – and that is virtually all of us in today's society.

In order to provide some context, I will first review two philosophers' theories of justice: Rawls (justice as fairness) and Nozick (entitlement theory). I will then explore technology as a significant factor in considering issues of justice, leading to the topic of teaching justice as a normative criterion in technological design decisions. As will be shown, this pedagogical approach is incorporated directly into the technical instruction, rather than using an add-on module, because in order "to improve a student's moral reasoning and sensitivity to ethical issues, engineering ethics must be integrative, delivered at multiple points in the curriculum, and incorporate specific discipline context."[1]

In teaching this topic, it is important that one not only establish knowledge of the relationship between justice and technology in students, but also encourage students to action. I will close with a few case studies as examples and a discussion of pedagogical and curricular tools that can help in teaching justice and technology.

Distributive Justice

Justice as Fairness: Rawls

John Rawls, in his book *A Theory of Justice*, promotes the idea of justice as fairness. Rather than exploring the origin of justice (considering the source of the notion that we should be just in our treatment of each other), he posits a thought experiment. Imagine a group of humans that is to decide on principles of justice for all. The group is in an "original position," kept behind a "veil of ignorance" preventing them from knowing ahead of time what their own particular place and position in society would be (i.e., they do not know the social class of their family, what their own innate abilities will be, what their prospects will be, etc.). In this state Rawls considers what principles they might develop. He supposes that they will adopt a "maximin" approach, which considers the worst-case scenario that one might find oneself in after adopting a set of principles. That is, Rawls suggests that this group of humans would select principles to maximize the prospects of the worst-off in society. He sums up his ideas by saying: "All social values – liberty and opportunity, income and wealth, and the bases of self-respect – are to be distributed equally unless an unequal distribution of any, or all, of these values is to everyone's advantage."[2]

Rawls addresses a number of the possible objections to his theory. One difficulty arises because the welfare of the least well-off dictates decisions regarding justice. This is the case no matter the scale of the difference: "Yet it seems extraordinary that the justice of increasing the expectations of the better placed by a billion dollars, say, should turn on whether the prospects of the least favored increase or decrease by a penny."[3] Rawls dismisses this difficulty by stating that it will not actually occur: "The possibilities which the objection envisages cannot arise in real cases; the feasible set is so restricted that they are excluded."[4] Rawls assumes a self-sufficient society, but with globalization effects (partly caused by technology), we must consider society to stretch across the globe. It might actually be the case that the justice of a billion-dollar difference in an ultra-wealthy Western businessman's fortune turns on the difference of merely pennies for a third-world subsistence farmer.

Entitlement Theory: Nozick

Robert Nozick notes at least two difficulties in Rawls' theory of justice. First, he questions Rawls' assumption that resources are "up for grabs" and should be distributed. This is problematic because most resources are currently owned or claimed by someone. Nozick makes the initially plausible claim that any situation that arises by just exchanges starting from an originally just distribution will also be just.[5] He thus proposes that principles of justice should cover how one justly acquires resources not yet owned, and how one then justly exchanges or transfers these resources.

Secondly, Nozick suggests that Rawls does not properly recognize the autonomy of the individual. He claims that the individual is sacrosanct and has rights that can only be limited at the boundary of the rights of another individual.[6] In fact, Rawls does describe the goal of extensive liberty for each in precisely these terms. However, the suggestion by Rawls that one's resources might be distributed to others appears to violate the individual's rights, in the eyes of Nozick.[7] He thus proposes his own thought experiment. Suppose a famous basketball player agrees to play for a certain team, but only if the team pays him a bonus that amounts to a surcharge on each ticket sold. The team agrees because this big star will draw a big crowd. Each person buying a ticket gladly pays the small surcharge because each wants to see the star play. If everyone started out with a just share of resources, then would we claim afterward that the big star has unjustly gained resources? Nozick claims that everyone got what they deserved: justice was served. Everyone attending the game wished to exchange their resources for the chance to see the star play. Does justice prevent individuals from using their own resources because this would result in an unequal distribution? Yet this is apparently the conclusion one would draw from Rawls.

Inadequacy of Rawls and Nozick

Both Rawls and Nozick develop principles of justice independent of an explicit religious framework. However, when a creator God is part of one's worldview, one sees the principles and requirements of justice in a new light. Because humans are created in God's image, Nozick's insistence on the importance of individuals seems appropriate, but not his assertion of autonomy. Rawls' attention to the least well-off when evaluating the justice of a situation comports well with God's special concern for the poor.

However, the thought experiment with which Rawls begins implies that humans have an a priori claim on those resources, when in fact we are merely stewards – God is the original distributor, not us.

A Christian worldview is informed by biblical principles, and the Bible provides a number of examples (and counterexamples) of justice. Interestingly, it is difficult to find much support for the claim that God intends for us to distribute all resources in precisely equal quantities. There are no obvious calls for the state (or anyone else for that matter) to redistribute goods according to some pattern of equality. Granted, there are redistributions, such as the year of Jubilee (Lev 25; 27) or the selling of personal property by early believers to aid the needy (Acts 2:44-45), but these are either not precisely equal redistributions or not imposed by outside authority. God does call us to care for the poor, to avoid wealth obtained by unjust means, and to be fair in our dealings with rich and with poor. For example, Isaiah 58:3 indicts God's people for exploiting workers. Micah 6:8 tells us that God requires humans to act justly. Prohibitions against partiality are plentiful, including Leviticus 19:15 and Deuteronomy 16:19. Proverbs 11:1 calls for accuracy in scales used for business transactions. It appears that a balance of distribution is required between Rawls and Nozick – neither a precise equality of all goods nor a neglect of the needs of the unfortunate.

Technology as Resource

Resources that we might consider for distribution under Rawls or as entitlements under Nozick include money, precious metals such as gold, timber, real estate, automobiles, clean drinking water, yachts, televisions, and food. Can the problem of just distribution be reduced to simply distribution of monetary wealth? Not completely. Money is often related to, but not synonymous with, power and influence. Money cannot buy everything. Except perhaps for the ultra-wealthy, even the well-off cannot create and maintain certain large-scale technological infrastructures, such as a highway system, an electrical power grid, or the Internet. Technology often requires an educational infrastructure that takes time as much as money. Thus technology forms a subset of those resources that we might consider the subject of (distributive) justice.

By technology I mean products produced from raw or engineered materials for practical purposes using math, science, and engineering know-how, as well as the finely tuned processes, methods, and activities that produce these products. Technology is practical in the sense that it is a tool – a means to an end, not an end in itself. Though one could broaden this definition to include even simple tools improvised in the moment of need, my definition focuses on modern technology that utilizes specific knowledge domains. My definition is somewhat different from that used in *Responsible Technology*, a book written by a Calvin Center for Christian Scholarship team around twenty years ago. The authors defined technology as a cultural activity and called the result of this activity a "technological artifact."[8] This usage seems awkward, when the common vocabulary uses the word *technology* to mean the artifact (objects or processes), rather than the actions that produce it. That is, common usage makes technology the product of an activity. Engineering produces technology just as writing, composing, and baking produce literature, music, and cookies. *Responsible Technology* also defines technology as a response to God. While this is true, it is not unique to technological activity – all of life is a response to God. Despite these minor criticisms, the definition of technology in terms of its cultural context and as a response is a valuable idea. Technology does not appear in a vacuum but is embedded in culture and society, thus having particular values and biases that must be considered, particularly in light of Christian responsibility to honor and glorify God.

Having defined technology and classified it as both a tool and a resource, we can now consider its relationship to justice. How can technology be unjust? Can technology cause injustice? Consider a bottle of aspirin. Can we not hold manufacturers responsible if they produce a defective product that actually makes people sick? Consider an automobile that has a defective gas tank, one that tends to explode when the vehicle is rear-ended. Could we not hold the manufacturer responsible? If the defect is due to a flaw in the design, could we not hold the designer of the vehicle responsible as well? If the gas tank is intentionally designed to produce an inexpensive vehicle targeted to the less well-off, so that the working poor are more likely to be injured by the design that the wealthy, then the technology – by design – is unjust. Even if any negative effects are unintentional (a flaw, or an unintended side-effect), the design could be unjust. Injustice need not be intentionally caused, though intent may increase culpability.

One could argue that the wealthy will always be able to buy more safety than the poor. But is this really the case? Should it be? In a capitalist economy, money can buy more of most commodities, including resources related to housing, health, education, and much more. It may be helpful to differentiate between resources that are necessities for life and resources that are luxuries. When divided into these categories, one could speak of injustice when not all persons have the necessities of life, and at the same time allow for luxuries in unequal shares without claiming injustice. It is difficult to pin down exactly which resources fall in the category of "necessary for life," but we might consider the lowest level of Maslow's hierarchy of needs – physiological needs such as food, water, air, and activity.[9] We might also include Maslow's next level – safety and security needs.[10]

The approach of dividing resources into two categories falls between Rawls and Nozick. It is weaker than Rawls, in that those with a large number of resources have more room for just changes in their fortune as long as the least well-off have the necessities. It is stronger than Nozick, in that the well-off have some responsibility to distribute their wealth if there are some in society without necessities. Following Rawls, justice would require distribution of resources deemed necessities. Today's global society (produced in large part through technology) brings virtually every corner of the globe within our purview. Justice demands that the wealthy consider the poor across the entire planet, now that technology has interconnected us so. Additionally, justice would allow that all other resources (beyond necessities) be entitlements similar to Nozick, in that persons could give them to others as gifts, earn them by labor or merit, and so forth.

Thus far, I have argued that justice includes equitable distribution of some resources – those that are necessities. Furthermore, I have asserted that technology plays a significant part in the distribution of those resources and that it is itself a resource. However, these two claims still could leave technology as a neutral party, simply a pawn that does not inherently affect the claims of justice. To claim that the technology itself is unjust, as in the case of tainted medicine or a defective gas tank design, is to declare technology non-neutral.

The neutrality of technology often goes unquestioned – consider the motto: guns don't kill people, people kill people. Moving students in a technical discipline to question such claims is a significant pedagogical challenge.[11] Many students hold steadfastly to the largely unexamined claim that technology is neutral. For example, a student once noted, "With a hammer I can either pound nails or commit murder – it is entirely my choice. The hammer cannot choose. Therefore the hammer is neutral." The student believes the tool wielder may be biased or unethical, but the tool itself is neutral, practically inconsequential to the questions of morality. This resistance to critical evaluation of the technology itself may be in part the result of a consumerist attitude that encourages thoughtless accumulation of technology as consumer product. Students also confuse neutrality with agency. It is true that technology has no agency – it cannot make an ethical choice. But neither is it a neutral tool. People with hammers are much more likely to pound. People with guns are much more likely to kill than those without. Technology expands one's choices and increases the scope of one's agency. Technology amplifies ability and power in particular ways that are shaped by design decisions. That amplification can be distorted or directed toward unjust ends. If an injustice occurs, we can often lay blame on the user of the technology, but the designer, manufacturer, distributor, and regulator may also bear some responsibility. Imagine a manufacturer of aspirin that uses manufacturing equipment that is difficult to clean. They design the equipment to reduce costs, knowing that this could easily result in tainted medicine. If a consumer gets sick from the aspirin, would we not hold the manufacturer responsible? Would we not reject the claim that the equipment is completely neutral with no culpability on the part of the manufacturer? Imagine a manufacturer of automobiles that designs a car with a vulnerable gas tank in order to reduce costs. If people are more likely to die in rear-end collisions as a result, would we not hold the manufacturer responsible? My focus is on the designer (the engineer) and, to a lesser degree, the manufacturer. Their responsibility can only be traced by a line that runs through the technological product itself.

So my claim is that technology is biased and that this bias can lead to injustice. Technological products are never neutral. At the very least, the engineer designs them to perform their intended tasks, and thus biases them toward that use. For example, the form of well-designed technology implies the function. Consider the form of the input ring on the front face of the Apple iPod, which implies that the user should swirl their finger to give a scrolling command, or consider the form of the hard striking surface of a hammer along with the handle, which implies pounding. The designer builds in the intended consequences of technology. However, technology also holds unintended consequences. An object's designs may hide flaws. It may contain additional function beyond what the designer imagined. Engineers bring their own cultural proclivities, faults, and blind spots to the technology design process. They – perhaps unwittingly – build a part of themselves into the design. Not only the beauty but also the flaws of the design reflect on the designer. We cannot always foresee all the interactions that may occur. For example, road rage has become a dangerous and sometimes deadly problem in America. What is it about our broader culture and the technology of the automobile that causes some to snap in uncontrollable anger? The answer is perhaps related to the anonymity and isolation that a car provides. How do we educate designers and users of technology to recognize complex effects like this? Let me now turn to one possible approach.

Design Norms

Engineers are the professionals who design technology. They design the technological products, the manufacturing process to produce the product, the packaging of the product, and more. Engineers are not scientists, though they frequently use the results of science; engineering applies science, but it is not simply applied science. Scientists discover what exists, while engineers create what has never existed before. While the scientific and engineering approach are both creative in the sense of being imaginative (one proposes alternative hypotheses about how nature works and the other proposes alternative solutions to a problem), they differ because engineering is also creative in the sense of being productive – it produces physical artifacts (technology). Engineers must excel at making decisions under constraint, and the nature of these constraints is very broad: "within the context of professional engineering practice, one must consider a system that includes at least the following elements … the economic, political, ethical, and social constraints as boundary conditions that define the possible range of solutions for engineering problems and demand the interaction of engineers with the public."[12]

The book *Responsible Technology*, mentioned earlier, was seminal in a number of ways. One important idea it introduced was a set of normative principles ("norms" for short) that provide a framework for making design decisions that honor biblical principles.[13] These norms have proven useful in teaching students how to honor their faith through their vocation in engineering. For example, student teams taught the norms as part of a design curriculum tend to point back to the norms in team reports and course evaluations when asked how their faith affected their design process. A set of design norms that I use (a list differing slightly from *Responsible Technology*) includes cultural appropriateness, transparency, integrity, justice, stewardship, caring, and humility. Technology designed for cultural appropriateness recognizes that people and communities have a history and tradition. In order to respect the culture into which the engineer introduces new technology, one must appropriately balance size, scale, specialization, centralization, and so forth. Transparent technology is open and understandable to the user. It is reliable, consistent, and trustworthy. Integrity is a norm that calls for the engineer to design for completeness – a harmony of form and function. Design with integrity also promotes human relationships. By considering the whole context, the design encourages positive interactions between people. Engineers honor the norm of stewardship by using resources frugally and thoughtfully, including both the resources consumed in the production of the technology (e.g., the steel and plastic in a hybrid automobile) and the resources consumed by the technological product itself (e.g., the gasoline to run the automobile). A caring design recognizes the whole person in each stakeholder (i.e., all those affected by the design) and takes into account the physical, the social, the psychological. Caring design produces technology not for its own sake but to better the lives of others. Engineers can be personally humble, but this humility ought to infuse their technology as well, by recognizing our own human limitations as well as the effects of sin. Humble designs provide safeguards and appropriate feedback to reduce or prevent harm from unforeseen circumstances or abuse of the technology.

Justice as a design norm includes several aspects. As a starting position, technological designs must meet standard engineering codes and legal requirements. However, because technology influences the balance and availability of certain basic resources that we deem necessities, justice as a design norm reaches much further. Technology influences virtually every basic resource that can be considered necessary. For example, technology affects access to clean drinking water. Dams, levies, and other civil engineering projects can redirect the flow of water, create lakes, or reduce water levels. Filtering technology can produce potable water from otherwise poor sources. A large bottled water facility could pump thousands of gallons of water out of a local water table and then transport it out of the area. Although inequitable distribution of water could certainly occur without the aid of technology, technology amplifies these effects. (Indeed, the amplification effect of technology has been discussed repeatedly in the philosophy of technology literature.[14]) We can easily find analogous influences of technology on other necessities beside water, including food, energy, shelter, employment, education, health care, and security.

In teaching engineering students to apply the design norm of justice, the instructor asks them to consider the various possible solutions to a posed engineering design problem, judging each solution by how it fares against design criteria, including the justice criterion. This engagement of justice to inform design choices can be part of a class activity, but it is even more effective when incorporated into student projects. This is not a trivial exercise, for not even experienced professionals, much less students, are able to foresee all the impacts of their designs. Judging a design based on the injustice it might produce requires discernment, wisdom, and a broad contextual education. This, of course, is one of the strengths of an engineering education at a college that emphasizes the liberal arts. Our engineering program at Calvin College benefits greatly from the strong liberal arts environment the college provides; engineering students educated in broad contextual disciplines are better prepared to consider the requirements of justice.

Example Case Studies

A few brief case studies provide some examples of applying the norm of justice to technology: the digital divide, energy scarcity, computer benchmarks, and health care. These examples show how to frame a technical topic as a question of justice. Case studies like this can be used in a class discussion within an engineering course.

The digital divide is the difference in access to information technology across spectrums of race, education, income, and other social classifications. One might expect that more educated or wealthier individuals would have better access to information technology. If information technology is a luxury, then the gap in access might be acceptable using the understanding of distributive justice discussed earlier. However, if access is a necessity, then this gap is an injustice. More disturbing than a difference in access based on income, a difference in access based on race is more difficult to explain or justify. For example, one recent study found that "the Digital Divide is large and does not appear to be disappearing soon. Blacks and Latinos are much less likely to have access to home computers than are white, non-Latinos.... Income differences are partly, but not entirely responsible for ethnic and racial disparities in computer and Internet access."[15] This difference rises to the level of injustice because information technology is becoming essential for finding employment, finding information on health care, accessing legal and governmental aid, and so forth. Why is there such a difference in information technology access based on race? Even after controlling for income and education, a racial gap in access still exists.[16] One might argue that we need not worry – the gap may be temporary, since there has been some evidence that this gap is closing for some groups. For example, a Canadian study found that middle-income groups were closing the gap in access compared to upper-income groups (though the gap with lower-income groups was actually widening).[17] A European study found that gender and age gaps are closing, but an income gap remains.[18] Even if this divide has been a temporary effect as much of society transitions to an information-based economy, the fact that this difference appeared and was statistically significant over a number of years is cause for concern. The design norm of justice calls us to analyze more carefully the reasons for the difference. Are there characteristics of the computer and the infrastructure of information technology that are racially biased or discriminatory in ways that are not obvious? Can we address this issue through changes in technology, governmental policy, or other means? A teacher can pose these questions to students in a class discussion, allowing them to struggle with some of the complex justice issues related to technology.

Much of our modern high-tech society runs on energy – sometimes enormous quantities of it. As the world supply of fossil fuel dwindles, it will become increasingly important to focus our society and our technology toward less energy-intensive lifestyles and toward alternative (preferably renewable) energy sources. Justice comes into play because North Americans cannot ask rapidly developing countries such as China and India to curb their energy use (and forgo the economic boon of cheap energy) when the looming shortage is due to Americans' massive ongoing use. Domestically, we also cause particular hardship for the working poor when fuel costs rise dramatically due to tight supplies. We should cultivate thinking outside the box in our classrooms, encouraging our students to think creatively about technologies that use less energy or use renewable sources. I have been encouraged at the increasing number of engineering senior design projects at Calvin College and elsewhere that have a focus on energy issues. At the same time, we must persuade students in all disciplines that business as usual in America cannot afford to continue in its high-energy ways.

A modern example of inaccurate scales (proscribed in Prov 11:1) might be computer benchmarks. Students in a computer engineering course can learn through a short project assignment that it can be challenging to get an apples-to-apples comparison of computer performance. In fact, such comparisons between different computer systems typically require complex, nuanced analysis and interpretation – leaving ample opportunity to thumb the scales unfairly and undetected. This project asks each student to select a computer to benchmark. Engineering students often have access to a great variety of different computers, so typically each student can find a distinct machine to test. The instructor dictates a particular benchmark program to use and may purposely choose a biased benchmark such as the Dhrystones program, which overemphasizes one particular type of computation (CPU integer performance). Once the students have returned their benchmark results to the instructor, the performance results from each student are combined (typically in a shared spreadsheet), and the students are asked to analyze the data in a second phase of the project. Through this assignment the students learn that benchmark results often do not represent the performance of a computer for most common applications, can be easily manipulated, and thus must be carefully interpreted. One might question whether benchmarking is relevant anymore since computer performance is outpacing our ability to use it. However, performance is still the primary selection criterion for purchasing a computer (whether a home machine for entertainment or a workstation for business). This makes performance a primary design criterion as well, and so bench-

marking remains an important and expected part of a computer engineering curriculum. One effective conclusion to a benchmarking project
like this is to have students evaluate advertisements for computers, hunt-
ing for examples of performance claims that are questionable.

As a final example, think about how modern health care depends so
heavily on technology. Few other sectors of our economy have seen
more explosive growth in high tech than here, and nowhere else are the
advantages of wealth more evident. For example, Viagra raked in over
$1.7 billion in 2002 for its manufacturer,[19] double the amount spent on
drugs to fight AIDS in Africa that same year.[20] However, high tech can
also help level the playing field, such as when remote telepresence
allows a doctor to meet "virtually" with widely dispersed patients in rural
areas. Using a collection of facts and news articles, a class can be
divided into two groups to debate issues related to health technology, for
example for and against statements such as "High-tech medical equipment and health care rightfully go to those that can afford it." Such
debates quickly tease out the underlying justice issues.

Teaching Justice and Technology: Pedagogical and Curricular Tools

This section provides some classroom methods and techniques for
teaching about justice and technology. Pedagogical tools such as engagement activities, class discussion, project assignments, and grading techniques are explored first, followed by a brief analysis of curriculum to support teaching justice.

As discussed earlier, teaching justice in relation to technology entails
challenging students to recognize the bias in technology. Engaging students on the topic of non-neutrality of technology can be difficult. Many
students find the topic too abstract or else they have strongly held convictions that technology is strictly neutral. Asking students to participate
in a concrete demonstration can help break the ice on this topic. One
activity that has been an effective tool in my classroom is to bring in a
large sack (such as a paper grocery bag) with two tools inside, hidden
from view. I then set a small wooden board on the desk that has two nails
partially embedded in the wood. Part way into a discussion of whether
technology is neutral, I ask for two volunteers. Each volunteer must fin-
ish pounding one of the nails into the board. The first student will represent a user who believes technology is not neutral – that it has certain
biases. By going first, this student has a choice about which tool to use
from the sack in order to accomplish the task. The second student represents a user who believes technology is strictly neutral and any biases

are in the user, not the tool. By going second, this student must use whatever tool remains in the sack to pound the second nail. The two tools in the sack are a hammer and a screwdriver. The first student has an easy time pounding with the hammer, while the second struggles (usually with humorous effect) to make any progress on the second nail using the screwdriver. Students will protest that the screwdriver is not meant for that task and no one would intentionally use a tool for such an obviously incompatible task. This opens the door for a deeper discussion on design intent, user understanding, and bias (intentional and unintentional) in technology. Other methods that effectively engage students in the debate over the neutrality of technology include a class discussion on the topic of tainted medicine (which easily leads into the concepts of responsibility, negligence, and accountability for all stakeholders), a dramatic presentation of the a case study such as the collapse of a TV transmission tower,[21] or a class debate on whether it is true that "guns don't kill people, people kill people" (which provides a good basis for explaining the difference between agency and neutrality).

Students are often more comfortable with concrete concepts, while faculty favor more abstract thinking. This can cause a disconnect when discussing important but abstract topics such as justice. Engineering students in particular often migrate toward numerical, objective methods. Embedding value judgments about justice directly into the technology design process can help make the connection between justice and technology less tenuous for students. This embedding can be done by broadening a technology design approach familiar to most engineering students: the design matrix. The design matrix is a table that lists various potential solutions to a problem in rows and criteria for evaluating those solutions as columns. For example, if the problem we are solving is that the interior environment of an automobile is too noisy for the passengers, we might list solutions in rows such as (a) building more noise-absorbing materials in to the interior surfaces, (b) providing heavier noise-blocking materials between the engine and the interior, or (c) adding noise-canceling electronics to the car radio. The decision criteria in the columns might include (1) cost, (2) effectiveness at reducing noise, and (3) effect on the safety of the vehicle. The design team then judges how well each potential solution in the rows meets the criteria of the columns, filling in a numerical score in each box of the table to reflect their judgment. The solution with the highest sum over all criteria represents the best solution to the problem. However, this is too simplistic, as different criteria do not have the same significance. Thus, the criteria are typically weighted and sometimes given a certain required minimum value below which proposed solutions are not considered. Students that favor numerical methods commonly use and appreciate the design matrix approach. A natural extension of the matrix adds the criterion of justice as a new column. This forces the team to evaluate each alternative solution in the light of justice. Will the proposed technology cause an inequity for certain stakeholders? Will it unfairly distribute some resource? Will it discriminate against a certain gender or race? Feedback and revision may be necessary for many teams that may not see any issues of justice in their selected projects, at least not initially. Some gentle nudging or a careful critique from the instructor may be required to open the eyes of students to the ramifications of their design choices.

A class activity that can be effective in generating good discussion on the concept of stakeholders as it relates to technology and justice is the "newspaper stakeholder hunt." The instructor splits the students into teams of two or three. Each team is given a recent newspaper (e.g., the *Wall Street Journal* or the *New York Times*) and asked to search the paper for examples of (a) problems that could be solved by technology or (b) technology that is solving a problem. For either case, they must then identify all potential stakeholders. This exercise helps them to see that technology affects many people. They must then consider whether justice (considered as equity or as respect or as particular rights) is honored for all stakeholders.

Should the teacher's role be restricted to imparting knowledge, without concern for behavior? Or should we strive to educate students so that they change their behavior? That is, should education for justice move head knowledge to heart knowledge? Where moral virtue is concerned, it is not enough simply to journey along educationally through Bloom's *Taxonomy* for the cognitive domain, making our way from early education objectives such as knowledge and comprehension to higher levels of learning such as synthesis and evaluation.[22] Like faith, knowledge of justice without resulting works is dead. Narrowly focusing education upon only the cognitive domain is particularly a problem in the technical disciplines, which often do not consider the affective domain to be relevant. Yet application of technical principles and ideas will always produce moral questions because application always involves moral choices. To teach justice means also to journey through Bloom's *Taxonomy* in the affective domain.[23]

Children learn more from their parents' actions than from their words. Likewise, students are very sensitive to whether teachers practice what they preach. Thus, it is important that all aspects of the classroom environment honor justice. For example, students must perceive that the grading system is equitable. If the grades do not seem fair, then the instructor loses credibility to speak on the subject of justice. In addition, use of justice as a normative criterion must be a graded portion of projects and assignments because students often assume that the most important concepts taught in a course are those that carry credit (appearing on an exam or part of a grading rubric for a project).

The typical curriculum in technical disciplines is not conducive to education on the topic of justice. Typical technical textbooks use canned problems with canned answers; that is, the problems are narrowly construed so that there is a single "correct" answer that can be deduced unambiguously. These types of problems not only teach the wrong set of technical skills but also discourage contextual thinking. They leave out all the "unnecessary" information, presumably in order to focus the students' attention on the important features of the problem. However, this approach is not realistic and in fact subtly conveys that only the technical details are important. Instead, students need to work through open-ended problems or large, complex class projects that contain all the messy details of real life – all the facts and opinions and ambiguity and interpretations and principles, without the benefit of the author telling them beforehand what is significant and what is extraneous. The need for "deeper inquiry and open-ended problem solving"[24] is clear in the literature, though it is also clear that students must "have some background in the primary technical area required of the project."[25] In open-ended problems, the student is taught that context matters: "Today's engineer must design under – and so understand at a deep level – constraints that include global, cultural, and business contexts."[26] The student and teacher can struggle together to find good trade-offs where no solution is perfect. Here is where the questions of justice can arise naturally rather than being added on artificially, as if they were an aside to the real problem. Of course this approach is more time-intensive; it is more difficult to grade thirty unique solutions than thirty identical solutions. The open-ended problem approach can be incorporated naturally into project courses, which are common as capstone experiences for senior engineering students. It takes come additional effort to incorporate them into the technical courses leading up to the senior year. One way is to use mini-projects within the course – more than simple textbook problems, but less than full-blown, semester-long projects.

Conclusion

In closing, I note that technology designers, technology users, and students of technology sometimes believe that technology itself is completely neutral, neither influenced by nor having influence on society. Not true. Technology is biased from inception and greatly influenced by the cultural context of the designer, manufacturer, distributor, and user. If we do not recognize that technology is biased, then we are ill prepared to deal with the consequences of those biases, some of which lead to injustice. On the other hand, if we identify the various influences and biases of technology, we can work to enhance justice through the tools we produce. We can teach students of engineering and science to recognize justice issues in what at first appear to be purely technical problems. Identifying such issues requires not only a strong technical foundation but a broad con-textual education as well. God calls us to act justly. Christian engineers who design technology have the specific responsibility to design their products with an eye toward justice. Christian teachers of engineers have a specific responsibility to teach their students how to design for justice.

Acknowledgments

I would like to thank Charles C. Adams and Gayle E. Ermer as well as several anonymous reviewers for their thoughtful advice as I prepared this paper.

Notes

1   Drake, Matthew J. et al., "Engineering Ethical Curricula: Assessment and Comparison of Two Approaches" in *Journal of Engineering Education* (April 2005) p. 223.

2   Rawls, John, *A Theory of Justice* (Cambridge, MA: Harvard Univ. Press, 1971) p. 62.

3   Rawls (1971) p. 157.

4   Rawls (1971) p. 158.

5   Nozick, Robert, *Anarchy, State, and Utopia* (New York: Basic Books, 1974) p. 151.

6   Nozick (1974) p. ix.

7   Nozick (1974) p. 163.

8   Monsma, Stephen V. (ed.), *Responsible Technology: A Christian Perspective* (Grand Rapids, MI: Eerdmans, 1986) p. 19.

9   Maslow, A. H., "A Theory of Human Motivation" in *Psychological Review*, 50:4 (1943) p. 372.

10   Maslow (1943) p. 376.

11   VanderLeest, Steven H., "The Built-in Bias of Technology" in *Proceedings of the 2004 American Society for Engineering Education (ASEE) Conference*, Salt Lake City, UT (June 2004) pp. 1418-1419.

12   National Academy of Engineering, *Educating the Engineer of 2020: Adapting Engineering Education to the New Century* (Washington, DC: The National Academies Press, 2005) p. 18.

13 Monsma (1986) pp. 170-177.

14 Mitcham, Carl, *Thinking through Technology: The Path between Engineering and Philosophy* (Chicago: Univ. of Chicago Press, 1994) p. 77.

15 Fairlie, Robert W., "Are We Really A Nation Online? Ethnic and Racial Disparities in Access to Technology and Their Consequences" Report for the Leadership Conference on Civil Rights Education Fund, September 20, 2005, http://www.civilrights.org/issues/communication/digitaldivide.pdf (29 May 2006).

16 National Telecommunications and Information Administration "Falling through the Net: Toward Digital Inclusion" (2000), http://www.ntia.doc.gov/ntiahome/digitaldivide (19 September 2005).

17 Sciadas, G., "Unveiling the Digital Divide," Statistics Canada, Minister of Industry (October 2002) p. 17.

18 Commission of the European Communities, "eInclusion revisited: The Local Dimension of the Information Society," Brussels, SEC (2005) 206. Available online at http://ec.europa.eu/comm/employment_social/knowledge_society/eincl_local_en.pdf (7 June 2006).

19 *Pfizer 2003 Financial Report* (New York: Pfizer, 2003) p. 7.

20 Weiss, Rick, "AIDS Funding Is Still Insufficient, U.N. Says" in *Washington Post* (22 September 2003) p. A19.

21 Texas A&M University, "TV Antenna Tower Collapse," http://ethics.tamu.edu/ethics/tvtower/tv3.htm (2 May 2006).

22 Bloom, Benjamin, *Taxonomy of Educational Objectives: Handbook 1, Cognitive Domain* (New York: Longman, 1956).

23 Krathwohl, David, Benjamin S. Bloom & Bertram B. Masia, *Taxonomy of Educational Objectives: The Classification of Educational Goals. Handbook II: The Affective Domain* (New York: David McKay, 1964).

24 Fromm, Eli, "The Changing Engineering Educational Paradigm" in *Journal of Engineering Education* (April 2003) p. 113.

25 Starkey, John M., Satish Ramadhyani & Robert J. Bernhard, "An Introduction to Mechanical Engineering Design for Sophomores at Purdue University" in *Journal of Engineering Education* (October 1994) p. 3.

26 Dym, Clive L. et al., "Engineering Design Thinking, Teaching, and Learning" in *Journal of Engineering Education* (January 2005) p. 111.

Bibliography

Bloom, Benjamin, *Taxonomy of Educational Objectives: Handbook 1, Cognitive Domain* (New York: Longman, 1956).

Commission of the European Communities, "eInclusion revisited: The Local Dimension of the Information Society," Brussels, SEC (2005) 206. Available online at http://ec.europa.eu/ comm/employment_social/knowledge_society/eincl_local_en.pdf (7 June 2006).

Drake, Matthew J. et al., "Engineering Ethical Curricula: Assessment and Comparison of Two Approaches" in *Journal of Engineering Education* (April 2005) pp. 223-231.

Dym, Clive L. et al., "Engineering Design Thinking, Teaching, and Learning" in *Journal of Engineering Education* (January 2005) pp 103-120.

Fairlie, Robert W., "Are We Really A Nation Online? Ethnic and Racial Disparities in Access to Technology and Their Consequences" Report for the Leadership Conference on Civil Rights Education Fund, September 20, 2005, http://www.civilrights.org/issues/communication/digitaldivide.pdf (May 29, 2006)

Fromm, Eli, "The Changing Engineering Educational Paradigm" in *Journal of Engineering Education* (April 2003) pp. 113-121.

Krathwohl, David, Benjamin S. Bloom & Bertram B. Masia, *Taxonomy of Educational Objectives: The Classification of Educational Goals. Handbook II: The Affective Domain* (New York: David McKay, 1964)

Maslow, A. H., "A Theory of Human Motivation" in *Psychological Review*, 50:4 (1943) pp. 370-396.

Mitcham, Carl, *Thinking through Technology: The Path between Engineering and Philosophy* (Chicago: Univ. of Chicago Press, 1994).

Monsma, Stephen V. (ed.), *Responsible Technology: A Christian Perspective* (Grand Rapids, MI: Eerdmans, 1986).

National Academy of Engineering, *Educating the Engineer of 2020: Adapting Engineering Education to the New Century* (Washington, DC: The National Academies Press, 2005).

National Telecommunications and Information Administration "Falling through the Net: Toward Digital Inclusion," 2000, http://www.ntia.doc.gov/ntiahome/digitaldivide (19 September 2005).

Nozick, Robert, *Anarchy, State, and Utopia* (New York: Basic Books, 1974).

Pfizer 2003 Financial Report (New York: Pfizer, 2003).

Rawls, John, *A Theory of Justice* (Cambridge, MA: Harvard Univ. Press, 1971).

Sciadas, G., "Unveiling the Digital Divide," Statistics Canada, Minister of Industry, October 2002.

Starkey, John M., Satish Ramadhyani, Robert J. Bernhard, "An Introduction to Mechanical Engineering Design for Sophomores at Purdue University" in *Journal of Engineering Education* (October 1994) pp. 1-8.

Texas A&M University, "TV Antenna Tower Collapse," http://ethics.tamu.edu/ethics/tvtower/tv3.htm (2 May 2006).

VanderLeest, Steven H., "The Built-in Bias of Technology" in *Proceedings of the 2004 American Society for Engineering Education (ASEE) Conference*, Salt Lake City, UT, (June 2004) pp. 1417-1427.

Weiss, Rick, "AIDS Funding Is Still Insufficient, U.N. Says" in *Washington Post* (22 September 2003) p. A19.

JE&CB 10:2 (2006) 129–142   1366-5456

Louis B. Gallien and LaTrelle Jackson

Character Development from African-American Perspectives: Toward a Counternarrative Approach

THIS CHAPTER ARGUES that character education, if it is to be effective, must be responsive to the values and narratives of particular cultural groups. It looks in particular at the cultural counternarratives informing traditions of character formation in African-American communities, and argues that these can provide a basis for successful character education. By grounding character education in the history, literature, and cultural and religious values of African-Americans, we are more likely to integrate the psychological, spiritual, and academic development of the next generation of African-American youth.

Context

In 2002, a United States Department of Education representative stated that two major initiatives were to be given top priority for federal funding, as the current administration believes they will have the greatest positive impact on urban schools across the United States: school vouchers and character development programs. The issue of school vouchers is an immense Pandora's Box filled with latent economic and class ramifications, and is beyond the scope of this essay. Regarding character education, unless such curricula are constructed in a culturally responsive manner, the administration's goals of encouraging responsible citizenship combined with producing people of character will ultimately fail in primarily black urban areas. This is because they are not constructed to be congruent with African-American counternarratives based on values that have been faithfully transmitted to many African-American groups since slavery. In other words, character curricular programs designed mainly for black urban youth must be culturally mediated and responsive if the current administration's goals are to be achieved. We suggest that this cultural mediation should be steeped in the history, literature, and cultural and religious values of African-Americans throughout American history, and that these values can be translated into effective curricular practices on character.

A Counternarrative to the Development of Character

The formation of values in many black communities – mostly those that are non-assimilated or have little cultural contact with majority culture – are historically informed by West African tribal traditions, the values of which sharply contrast with those of Western culture, and especially with the fabled American metanarrative of rugged individualism, meritocracy, capitalism, materialism, and competition. There are an identifiable set of values and a history of enslaved African-Americans that form a counternarrative of character and value development, contrasting with American principles centered on life, liberty, and the pursuit of happiness, principles that were systematically denied to slaves and freed African-Americans until the twentieth century and yet were taught as nearly sacrosanct in our schools. As Carruthers argues, "[d]irectly attributable to schooling founded on European-centered constructions of knowledge, the crisis in Black education will not be resolved until Black intellectuals achieve intellectual freedom and re-construct Black education on an African-centered foundation. These are the pre-conditions to the real liberation of the African race all over the world."[1] Though many African-Americans believe that the principles derived from the American metanarrative are important, the attainment of those principles by free black people came through a different set of values, which their leaders learned from their own culture and the culture of other subjugated people of color (such as the influence of Gandhi on the life and thought of Dr. Martin Luther King, Jr.[2]).

There is a wealth of information stored in the various literatures, history, and traditions of African-American peoples that can inform and frame research models on how African-American communities have effectively and faithfully transmitted models of character to their youth. These stories, models, and histories need to be compiled in order to respond positively to President Bush's call for effective character development programs in the inner cities of the United States. A contemporary and instructive example of the African-American counternarrative is the case of Sallie Hemings, a slave of the third American president, Thomas Jefferson. Slave lore (i.e., oral tradition) faithfully transmitted in the slave community at Monticello stated that Jefferson was the father of several of Hemings's children. Certain members of the Caucasian branch of the Jefferson family became indignant when a few of Sallie's descendants arrived for the annual Jefferson reunion on the "ole plantation" a decade ago. After ensuing internal battles, DNA tests were incorporated to find out which narrative was accurate, and the Hemings legend is now part of *our* history. The point is this: *logos*-centered knowledge, which is highly valued in Western civilization, is finite. Oral traditions, as related in the Old Testament, can be faithful historical and cultural witnesses to the past and, as such, are valuable sources of historical knowledge.

Since slavery, African-Americans have constructed the aforementioned counternarrative for teaching about character development from healthy, African-inspired traditions and models of family living.[3] Many African-American groups look to historical and cultural markers for a belief system that sharply contrasts with the values of many European-American groups. Those principles are built upon the following emphases from African tribal traditions brought over to America as researched by Boykin: spirituality, harmony, movement, verve, affect, communalism, expressive individualism, oral tradition, and social time perspective.[4] Karenga's research complements Boykin's as he found the following principles in his research on African traditions: unity, self-determination, collective responsibility, cooperative economics, purpose, creativity, and faith.[5] Additionally, Joyce King has highlighted the following differences in her latest book on black education: a) the priority is on the African ethnic family over the individual; b) the "ways of knowing" provided by the arts and humanities are often more useful in forming an understanding of our lives and experiences and those of other oppressed people than the knowledge and methodologies of the sciences that have been privileged by the research establishment despite the distorted or circumscribed knowledge and understanding this way of knowing often produces; c) paradoxically, from the perspective of the education research establishment, knowledge production is viewed as the search for (universal) truth, whereas the circumstances of African-Americans' social and existential condition require the search for contextual knowledge, or knowledge that is grounded in a particular culture.[6] While not all African-American groups follow these principles, many who reside in the urban areas being singled out for character development by the Department of Education do abide by many of these centuries-old principles.[7]

Further, by utilizing African-American perspectives on character issues, combined with culturally responsive pedagogy, educators can have a positive impact on character education programs in urban areas. Since the end of the last century, the literature on effective teaching strategies for African-Americans has been replete with studies that have shown the efficaciousness of such methods. Teachers in urban areas are realizing that they can have a greater pedagogical effect on their African-

American students if they understand and acknowledge their culture and history. Teachers who are aware of the language patterns, cultural and historical traditions, religious orientations, and social norms of African-Americans relate more effectively to their students than those who have little or no knowledge of these important cultural markers.[8] Current research consistently demonstrates that teachers who relate well to African-American students have a greater positive academic impact than those without such background cultural knowledge.[9]

Contextual Literature Review

The literature on character education exhibits a dearth of knowledge regarding how African-Americans have transmitted their understanding of character throughout United States history.[10] Certainly, there are great works of literature and history written by authors who have described to teachers, parents, pastors, and others the complexities in coming to terms with the different avenues for teaching character within their respective communities. But representations of character building are absent from the following fields: educational history, church history, black history and literature from a gendered and racially-nuanced perspective, child and human development, social and political contexts, and perspectives from historically segregated/black institutions. An inter-disciplinary emphasis can engage further discussion and research on this subject and provide a better understanding of multiple perspectives on character education from specific cultural groups. This research may also bridge the current cultural disconnection between African-Americans and the educational goals of the current administration.[11]

On a K-12 curricular level, recommendations, pedagogical strategies and methods for teaching character to urban youth are needed to teach disaffected youth.[12] One of the better avenues for imparting character is through reading and discussing stories. Well-chosen stories are evocative for many people: they inspire groups and individuals to become people of character and purpose. By collecting stories from people of the same racial heritage, educators can be more focused and intentional about character development. As a result, they can encourage several curricular approaches to teaching character in context with African-American history and traditions.[13]

As Lawrence Blum noted: "Literature on moral education has contributed surprisingly little to our understanding of issues of race and education."[14] Lickona, Bennett, and Damon all say very little about racial differences in developing lives of moral character.[15] Their norms are taken from a very distinctive view of majority culture. Blum suggests that

African-American communities have taken a different trek to transmitting character and values to their young people. Borrowing from Martin Luther King Jr's term the "beloved community," he suggests that issues of character in the African-American community are inseparable from issues of justice. Just as Carol Gilligan and Robert Coles challenged their colleague Lawrence Kohlberg's notions of moral development by pointing out that his research had failed to take into consideration issues of gender and context, (and, for Coles, issues of spiritual transcendence), Blum suggests that character and moral values in African-American communities are transmitted not only by individuals but also by *communities* of justice who retell stories of courage and character endemic to the history of African-Americans.[16]

Coles's oft-cited study of Ruby Bridges is instructive in this area. Bridge's resilience in the face of overt racism and potential violence in New Orleans in the early 1960s caused Coles, a trained psychiatrist, to rethink moral development theories that had been based on the experiences of upper-middle-class white men. Bridge's gracious reaction to the racist epithets hurled at her suggested a much higher moral awareness than the current theories allowed, and Coles noticed that she was praying for her abusers. Therefore, the role of spiritual transcendence in an individual's moral development became the object of Coles's research for the next three decades in works like the *Spiritual Growth of Children, Harvard Diary,* and multiple journal articles on the integration of faith and learning. Much like C. S. Lewis's argument for the existence of God (i.e., to explain the existence of supernatural events one would first have to explore the origins of the term *super*), Coles believed that one must collect stories from another culture in order to come to terms with inclusive aspects of moral development.[17]

The Fragmented Threat to the Counternarrative: Civil Rights v. Hip-Hop Cultures

Character development within African-American communities is a complex and global process that must be historically and culturally mediated in a modern context, so that policy makers, community leaders, academicians, and mental health providers can contextualize moral or character education within a framework that leads to healthy "development." In many ways, character development is the dynamic interplay between internal determinants and external influences in order for positive growth to occur. Factors such as media influences,[18] acculturative stress,[19] and racial identity[20] significantly impact the development outcomes and success potential of African-Americans.

African-American youth are faced with conflicting messages of how to achieve that pit their inherited values of spirituality, solidarity, and service (derived from the counternarrative) against values coming from the current hip-hop, postmodern and nihilistic narratives built on power, property, and pleasure.[21] Additionally, adolescence is a critical time of self-reflection and self-definition in which youths must work to determine what kind of persons they would like to become and how well they are meeting this goal.[22] In making these judgments, teens draw on their peers and cultural icons from the hip-hop movement both for visible role models and for peer approval. Prominent among these influential others are parents and peers, whose approval and support have been shown to be major contributors to teens' identity.[23]

Clearly, the current battle for the minds and hearts of African-American youth is centered on the friction between the civil rights generation of African-American leaders, whose values were grounded on communal solidarity, versus the current generation of commercial hip-hop role models, who base their values on a postmodern worldview that contrasts with the communal sacrifice to which black civil rights leaders called their people during the movement's ascendancy under Martin Luther King Jr.[24]

Hip-hop scholar Todd Boyd points out:

> This is why hip hop is so important: it forces us to move on by knocking down those obstacles from the past, by breaking all those rules, in order to get past this novocaine-like relationship that so many have to civil rights and recognize the more nuanced forms of racism that continue to dominate our society. To me, this transition from civil rights to hip-hop is akin to a line from an old Bohannon cut, "Wide Receiver": the first time we knocked on the door, this time we gonna kick it in![25]

Racial Self-Identity

At the beginning of the last century, W. E. B. Dubois argued that the central problem of American society was the color line.[26] An examination of the psychological literature over the past one hundred years suggests that Dubois was visionary in his assessment. Social psychology has been examining the meaning of race in the lives of African-Americans since its earliest inception. Some researchers have reported that African-Americans who identify strongly with being black may be at psychological risk as a result of the stigma associated with the identity.[27] Conversely, others suggest that a strong identification with one's race can serve as a protective buffer to personal self-esteem.[28] These two lines of identity indicate the complexity of how race is conceptualized and the *actual* relationship between racial identification and character development.

Cross originally presented a five-stage model (Pre-encounter, Encounter, Immersion/Emersion, Internalization, Internalization/ Commitment) of racial identity development in which each stage was characterized by self-concept issues concerning race as well as parallel attitudes about blacks and whites as reference groups.[29] Each stage, it was argued, provides a framework for how one thinks, feels, and behaves. Depending on one's stage, the individual would use either black or white representatives as the primary reference group. Helms amended Cross's work to include the consideration of one's cognitive maturational level and the interplay with societal influences.[30] According to the theory, progression from one stage to another is influenced by environmental factors and how one interprets these experiences. Interpretations of life's meaningful experiences have both internal (personal reflection) and external (information gathering, oral feedback exchanges) roots. Oral traditions have the power to facilitate meaning-making when seeking an answer to the question, who am I? Further, oral traditions promote a sense of direction in answering the next question, who can I become? Historically, these traditions were delivered via multiple sources, particularly within families, community centers, churches, and school systems. Although segregated communities were denied access to the best physical tools for learning, they promoted a sense of unity, identity, and drive toward a clear goal: a better tomorrow.[31] African-Americans not only taught their young the essence of cultural pride from a collectivistic standpoint, they also incorporated the roles of family discipline, dual consciousness, and self-management into their rearing practices. However, without the connection to the abiding values of one's culture, the training process is incomplete. Kunjufu stated that the traditional values of people of African descent have shifted from a framework of "we," cooperation, and internal foci to a contemporary value set rooted in American ideology targeting an "I" framework of competition and external rewards/validation.[32] This shift has had a tremendous impact on expressions of respect for the elders within the community, on musical genres, and on family functioning.

Clash of Cultures and Value-Conflict

For many African-Americans, the cultural counternarratives consisting of education, resilience, connectedness to fictive kin, black pride, and knowing one's place have diminished in salience. Naim Akbar asserted that "the cooperative that was the mainstay of traditional African societies and an instrument of survival in the slavery and oppressive environments of the West have been overwhelmed by the push for individualism."[33] Given that individualism is linked to Western value systems, and that some African-Americans have embraced these values through cultural assimilation, many believe that key cultural strengths have been internally sabotaged. In order for character development programs to be grounded in an Afrocentric worldview, Akbar and other noted psychologists suggest the educational system must restore the principle of *umoja* (collective work and responsibility). Programs that incorporate the principle of *umoja* such as Michigan State University professor Geneva Smitherman's "My Brother's Keeper" program have experienced longitudinal success. Some may argue that the hip-hop movement captures the essence of *umoja* by mobilizing a generation of youth rather than a cultural group of people.[34] Conversely, others question the implications of current trends within the movement and the possible negative influences for black youth identity, particularly that of black females. Some argue that the United States, though blessed with the richest resources in the world, has a generation that embraces a nihilistic, relativistic mindset and discounts historical occurrences as irrelevant to present-day human interactions.[35] This suggests that the need to restructure our child rearing and educational practices is greater than ever before. Educators, clinicians, parents, neighbors, and Christians need to provide access to cultural pathways so that students can begin answering their identity questions based on knowing collectively where they have been. Each of these groups can participate in the directional outcome of this quest in hopes of preventing the predictions noted in Isaiah 3:4-5 (NIV): "I will make boys their officials; mere children will govern them. People will oppress each other – man against man, neighbor against neighbor. The young will rise up against the old, the base against the honorable." Perhaps the prophet's words are still relevant today considering some of the top stories in the news.

Conclusion

So, how does one tackle the daunting task of character education reform with a special interest in African-Americans? As previously identified, the first step is awareness. Next, it is necessary to merge the stages of racial identity development with Afrocentric principles derived from the counternarrative that establishes a sturdy and developmentally appropriate framework for interventions. It is imperative that we promote legacy-building within a racial-identity-stage-sensitive framework for cultural knowledge acquisition and assimilation to occur. To be truly transforming, character education must be provided in a culturally-responsive context so that someone in the preencounter stage can glean insight into their own character development just as successfully as someone in the internalization stage of development. Then, we can validate the youthful desire for immediacy while teaching the value of historical contributions. Third, we must expose the more nihilistic and relativistic value base of the commercialized hip-hop movement to our African-American youth. We should not allow the current popularity (or the more insidious nature) of the culture to keep it from a critique of its implied and direct value base that threaten a counternarrative that has allowed black communities to thrive for three hundred years. Further, if we are to encourage healthy forms of indigenous character development within African-American communities, we must demonstrate how some of these commercialized values contain the seeds of communal decay and undermine black self-determination. Also, it is important that we understand character development as it has been historically understood in the black church. In the segregated era of black education, there was little recognition of the separation of church and state, therefore, the black church formed an important historical triangulation between neighborhood, church and schooling for a more seamless formation of character. Finally, it is necessary to tap into students' "zone of influence" for the cultural messages to be incorporated long term. Over the years this zone has changed from home, school, and church as primary influencers, to home, peers, and television.[36] With the onset of technological advances such as computers, blogs, and instant messaging, the scope of peer influence has multiple access points. Reform efforts must target the information-input sources when addressing moral education initiatives. By taking each of these components, educators, clinicians, parents, and neighbors can integrate the psychological, spiritual, and academic development of our next generation. For when we ensure strong character formation in our *children*, we ensure the potentials associated with our collective *future*.

Notes

1   Carruthers, J., *Black Intellectuals and the Crisis in Black Education: A Paradox of Black Life in White Societies* (Trenton, NJ: African World Press, 1994) p. 41.

2   King, J. (ed.), *Black Education: A Transformative Research and Action Agenda for the New Century* (Hillsdale, NJ: Erlbaum Press, 2005).

3   Ladner, J., *Timeless Values for African American Families* (New York: Wiley and Sons, 1998).

4   Boykin, A. W., "The Triple Quandary and the Schooling of Afro-American Children" in Neisser, U. (ed.), *The School Achievement of Minority Children* (Hillsdale, NJ: Erlbaum Press, 1985).

5   Karenga, M., *Kawaida Theory: An Introduction* (Inglewood, CA: Kawaida Press, 1980).

6   King (2005) pp. 20-21.

7   Patillo-McCoy, Mary, *Black Picket Fences* (Chicago: Univ. of Chicago Press, 1999); West, C., *Race Matters* (New York: Vintage Press, 1994).

8   Irvine. J. J., *In Search of Wholeness* (New York: Palgrave Press, 2002).

9   Delpit. L., *Other People's Children* (New York: New Press, 1995); Gay, G., *Culturally Responsive Teaching: Theory, Research, and Practice* (New York: Teachers College Press, 2000); Hale, J., *Unbank the Fire* (Baltimore: Johns Hopkins Press, 1994); Howard, G., *We Can't Teach What We Don't Know* (New York: Teachers College Press, 1999); Irvine, J. J., *Black Students and School Failure* (Westport, CT: Praeger Press, 1990); Ladson-Billings, G., *The Dreamkeepers: Successful Teachers of African American Children* (San Francisco: Jossey-Bass, 1994); Murrell, P., *African-Centered Pedagogy* (Albany, NY: SUNY Press, 2002).

10 Ryan, K. & T. Lickona (eds.), *Character Development in Schools and Beyond* (Washington, DC: Council for Research in Values and Philosophy, 1992).

11 Pollard, D. & C. Ajirotutu, *African-Centered Schooling in Theory and Practice* (Westport, CT: Bergin and Garvey Press, 2000).

12 Boykin, A. W., "The Triple Quandary and the Schooling of Afro-American Children" in Neisser, U. (ed.), *The School Achievement of Minority Children* (Hillsdale, NJ: Erlbaum Press, 1985); Pierce, W., E. Lemke & R. Smith, "Critical Thinking and Moral Development in Secondary Students" in *High School Journal*, 71 (1988); Piro, J. & J. Lorio, "Rationale and Responsibilities in the Teaching of Critical Thinking to American Schoolchildren" in *Journal of Instructional Psychology*, 17 (1991); Watts, R., J. Abdul-Adil & T. Pratt, "Enhancing Critical Consciousness in Young African American Men: A Psychoeducational Approach" in *Psychology of Men and Masculinity*, 3:1 (2002).

13 Coles, R., *The Call of Stories: Teaching and the Moral Imagination* (Boston: Houghton Mifflin Press, 1989).

14 Blum, L., "Race, Community, and Moral Education: Kohlberg and Spielberg as Civic Educators" in *Journal of Moral Education*, 28:2 (1999).

15 Lickona, T., *Educating for Character* (New York: Bantam Press, 1991); Bennett, W., *The Devaluing of America* (New York: Touchstone Books, 1992); Damon, W., *The Moral Child* (New York: Free Press, 1988).

16 Gilligan, Carol, *In a Different Voice* (Cambridge, MA: Harvard Univ. Press, 1982); Coles, Robert, *The Moral Life of Children* (New York: The Atlantic

Monthly Press, 1986); Kohlberg, Lawrence, *The Psychology of Moral Development* (New York: Harper Row, 1983).

17 Lewis, C. S., *Miracles* (Carmichael, CA: Touchstone Books, 1996).

18 Ward, M., "Wading Through the Stereotypes: Positive and Negative Associations Between Media Use and Black Adolescents' Conceptions of Self" in *Developmental Psychology*, 40:2 (2004).

19 Berry, J. W., U. Kim, T. Minde & D. Mok, "Comparative Studies of Acculturative Stress" in *International Migration Review*, 21 (1987).

20 Cross, William E., "Models of Psychological Nigrescence: A Literature Review" in Jones, R. (ed.), *Black Psychology*, 2nd ed. (New York: Harper & Row, 1980).

21 West (1994); Gallien, Louis, "Keeping it Real: Hip-Hop Culture and the Framing of Values for Contemporary African American Students" in *Journal of College and Character*, 2 (2006).

22 E.g., Erikson, E. *Identity: Youth and Crisis* (New York: Norton, 1968); Moshman, D., "Adolescent Psychological Development. Rationality, Morality, and Identity" in *Family Relations*, 43 (1999).

23 Harter, S., "The Development of Self-Representations" in Damon, W. & N. Eisenberg (eds.), *Handbook of Child Psychology: Vol. 3. Social, Emotional, and Personality Development*, 5th ed (New York: Wiley, 1998); Kunjufu, J., *To Be Popular or Smart* (Chicago: African American Images, 1988).

24 Boyd, Todd, *Am I Black Enough for You?* (Bloomington, IN: Indiana Univ. Press, 1997); Dyson, M. E. *The Michael Eric Dyson Reader* (NewYork: Basic Civitas Press, 2004).

25 Boyd, Todd, *The New H.N.I.C.: The Death of Civil Rights and the Reign of Hip-Hop* (New York: New York Univ. Press, 2003) p. 43.

26 Dubois, W. E. B., *Souls of Black Folk* (Chicago: A. C. McClurg, 1903).

27 E.g., Horowitz, R., "Racial Aspects of Self-Identification in Nursery School Children" in *Journal of Psychology*, 7 (1939); Kardiner, A., & L. Ovesey, *The Mark of Oppression* (New York: Norton, 1951); Steele, C. M. & J. Aronson, "Stereotype Threat and the Intellectual Performance of African Americans" in *Journal of Personality and Social Psychology*, 69 (1995).

28 E.g., Azibo, D. A., "African-Centered Theses on Mental Health and a Nosology of Black African Personality Disorder" in *Journal of Black Psychology*, 15 (1989); Baldwin, J. A., "African Self-Consciousness and the Mental Health of African Americans" in *Journal of Black Studies*, 15 (1984); Cross, William E., *Shades of Black: Diversity in African American Identity* (Philadelphia: Temple Univ. Press, 1991).

29 Cross, William E., "Negro-to-Black Conversion Experience" in *Black World*, 20 (1971).

30 Helms, J., "Expanding Racial Identity Theory to Cover Counseling Process" in *Journal of Counseling Psychology*, 33:1 (1986).

31 Siddle-Walker, V., *Their Highest Potential* (Chapel Hill, NC: UNC Press, 1996).

32 Kunjufu, J., *Countering the Conspiracy to Destroy Black Boys* (Chicago: Afro-American Images, 1984).

33 Akbar, Naim, *The Community of Self* (Tallahassee: Mind Productions and Associates, 1985), 71.

34 Boyd (2003); Kitwana, B., *Why White Kids Love Hip Hop: Wangstas, Wiggers, Wannabes, and the New Reality of Race in America* (New York: Basic Civitas Books, 2005).

35 Kilson, M., "The Pretense of Hip-Hop Black Leadership" in *The Black Commentator*, 50 (2003), http://www.blackcommentator.com/50/50_kilson_pf.html (17 July 2003).

36 Kunjufu, (1984).

Bibliography

Akbar, Naim, *The Community of Self* (Tallahassee: Mind Productions and Associates, 1985).

Azibo, D. A., "African-Centered Theses on Mental Health and a Nosology of Black African Personality Disorder" in *Journal of Black Psychology*, 15 (1989) pp. 173-214.

Baldwin, J. A., "African Self-Consciousness and the Mental Health of African Americans" in *Journal of Black Studies*, 15 (1984) pp. 177-194.

Bennett, W., *The Devaluing of America* (New York: Touchstone Books, 1992).

Berry, J. W., U. Kim, T. Minde & D. Mok, "Comparative Studies of Acculturative Stress" in *International Migration Review*, 21 (1987) pp. 491-511.

Blum, L., "Race, Community, and Moral Education: Kohlberg and Spielberg as Civic Educators" in *Journal of Moral Education*, 28:2 (1999) pp. 125-143.

Boyd, Todd, *Am I Black Enough for You?* (Bloomington, IN: Indiana Univ. Press, 1997).

Boyd, Todd, *The New H.N.I.C.: The Death of Civil Rights and the Reign of Hip-Hop* (New York: New York Univ. Press, 2003).

Boykin, A. W., "The Triple Quandary and the Schooling of Afro-American Children" in Neisser, U. (ed.), *The School Achievement of Minority Children* (Hillsdale, NJ: Erlbaum Press, 1985) pp. 57-92.

Boykin, A. W. & F. Tom, "Black Child Socialization: A Conceptual Framework" in McAdoo, H. & J. McAdoo (eds.), *Black Children* (Beverly Hills: Sage, 1985) pp. 33-51.

Carruthers, J., *Black Intellectuals and the Crisis in Black Education: A Paradox of Black Life in White Societies* (Trenton, NJ: African World Press, 1994).

Coles, Robert, *The Moral Life of Children* (New York: The Atlantic Monthly Press, 1986).

Coles, Robert, *The Call of Stories: Teaching and the Moral Imagination* (Boston: Houghton Mifflin Press, 1989).

Cross, William E., "Negro-to-Black Conversion Experience" in *Black World*, 20 (1971) pp. 13-27.

Cross, William E., "Models of Psychological Nigrescence: A Literature Review" in Jones, R. (ed.), *Black Psychology*, 2nd ed. (New York: Harper & Row, 1980) pp. 81-98.

Cross, William E., *Shades of Black: Diversity in African American Identity* (Philadelphia: Temple Univ. Press, 1991).

Damon, W., *The Moral Child* (New York: Free Press, 1988).

Delpit. L., *Other People's Children* (New York: New Press, 1995).

Dubois, W. E. B., *Souls of Black Folk* (Chicago: A. C. McClurg, 1903).

Dyson, M. E. *The Michael Eric Dyson Reader* (NewYork: Basic Civitas Press, 2004).

Erikson, E. *Identity: Youth and Crisis* (New York: Norton, 1968).

Gallien, Louis, "Keeping it Real: Hip-Hop Culture and the Framing of Values for Contemporary African American Students" in *Journal of College and Character*, 2 (2006) pp. 1-14.

Gay, G., *Culturally Responsive Teaching: Theory, Research, and Practice* (New York: Teachers College Press, 2000).

Gilligan, Carol, *In a Different Voice* (Cambridge, MA: Harvard Univ. Press, 1982).

Hale, J., *Unbank the Fire* (Baltimore: Johns Hopkins Press, 1994).

Harter, S., "The Development of Self-Representations" in Damon, W. & N. Eisenberg (eds.), *Handbook of Child Psychology: Vol. 3. Social, Emotional, and Personality Development*, 5th ed (New York: Wiley, 1998) pp. 553-617.

Helms, J., "Expanding Racial Identity Theory to Cover Counseling Process" in *Journal of Counseling Psychology*, 33:1 (1986) pp. 62-64.

Horowitz, R., "Racial Aspects of Self-Identification in Nursery School Children" in *Journal of Psychology*, 7 (1939) pp. 91-99.

Howard, G., *We Can't Teach What We Don't Know* (New York: Teachers College Press, 1999).

Irvine, J. J., *Black Students and School Failure* (Westport, CT: Praeger Press, 1990).

Irvine. J. J., *In Search of Wholeness* (New York: Palgrave Press, 2002).

Kardiner, A., & L. Ovesey, *The Mark of Oppression* (New York: Norton, 1951).

Karenga, M., *Kawaida Theory: An Introduction* (Inglewood, CA: Kawaida Press, 1980).

Kilson, M., "The Pretense of Hip-Hop Black Leadership" in *The Black Commentator*, 50 (2003), http://www.blackcommentator.com/50/50_kilson_pf.html (17 July 2003).

King, J. (ed.), *Black Education: A Transformative Research and Action Agenda for the New Century* (Hillsdale, NJ: Erlbaum Press, 2005).

Kitwana, B., *Why White Kids Love Hip Hop: Wangstas, Wiggers, Wannabes, and the New Reality of Race in America* (New York: Basic Civitas Books, 2005).

Kohlberg, Lawrence, *The Psychology of Moral Development* (New York: Harper Row, 1983).

Kunjufu, J., *Countering the Conspiracy to Destroy Black Boys* (Chicago: Afro-American Images, 1984).

Kunjufu, J., *To Be Popular or Smart* (Chicago: African American Images, 1988).

Ladner, J., *Timeless Values for African American Families* (New York: Wiley and Sons, 1998).

Ladson-Billings, G., *The Dreamkeepers: Successful Teachers of African American Children* (San Francisco: Jossey-Bass, 1994).

Lewis, C. S., *Miracles* (Carmichael, CA: Touchstone Books, 1996).

Lickona, T., *Educating for Character* (New York: Bantam Press, 1991).

Moshman, D., "Adolescent Psychological Development. Rationality, Morality, and Identity" in *Family Relations*, 43 (1999) pp. 342-348.

Murrell, P., *African-Centered Pedagogy* (Albany, NY: SUNY Press, 2002).

Patillo-McCoy, Mary, *Black Picket Fences* (Chicago: Univ. of Chicago Press, 1999).

Pierce, W., E. Lemke & R. Smith, "Critical Thinking and Moral Development in Secondary Students" in *High School Journal*, 71 (1988) pp. 120-126.

Piro, J. & J. Lorio, "Rationale and Responsibilities in the Teaching of Critical Thinking to American Schoolchildren" in *Journal of Instructional Psychology*, 17 (1991) pp. 3-12.

Pollard, D. & C. Ajirotutu, *African-Centered Schooling in Theory and Practice* (Westport, CT: Bergin and Garvey Press, 2000).

Ryan, K. & T. Lickona (eds.), *Character Development in Schools and Beyond* (Washington, DC: Council for Research in Values and Philosophy, 1992).

Siddle-Walker, V., *Their Highest Potential* (Chapel Hill, NC: UNC Press, 1996).

Steele, C. M. & J. Aronson, "Stereotype Threat and the Intellectual Performance of African Americans" in *Journal of Personality and Social Psychology*, 69 (1995) pp. 797-811.

Ward, M., "Wading Through the Stereotypes: Positive and Negative Associations Between Media Use and Black Adolescents' Conceptions of Self" in *Developmental Psychology*, 40:2 (2004) pp. 284-294.

Watts, R., J. Abdul-Adil & T. Pratt, "Enhancing Critical Consciousness in Young African American Men: A Psychoeducational Approach" in *Psychology of Men and Masculinity*, 3:1 (2002) pp. 41-50.

West, C., *Race Matters* (New York: Vintage Press, 1994).

JE&CB 10:2 (2006) 143–165   1366-5456

Bradford S. Hadaway

Preparing the Way for Justice: Strategic Dispositional Formation through the Spiritual Disciplines[1]

THOUGH MORAL EDUCATORS cannot make their students virtuous, they can promote certain habits of active learning, analogous to the traditional spiritual disciplines, which can dispose the soul towards the subsequent blossoming of embodied and lived-out justice. The incorporation of a range of these disciplines improves typical service learning courses because each discipline is designed to resist or prune preexisting negative dispositions which could otherwise undermine the transformative power of the service learning experiences themselves. Kant's doctrine of virtue and Merton's account of monastic spirituality are developed to explain and defend this view.

Introduction

Teachers of moral philosophy who believe there is some merit to the idea that the moral formation and transformation of their students is a worthwhile and legitimate pedagogical goal are often confronted with the realization that typical ethics courses are ill suited to this task.[2] At best in such "read and talk" courses, we hope that students will experience a kind of cognitive transformation as they encounter different theoretical constructs, learn reflective and critical thinking skills, and perhaps even discover arguments that might compel them to think differently about particular moral issues. With standard pedagogical methods in ethics, the thought that some student might actually leave class a morally better person seems more contingent upon the student's own desire and efforts at moral transformation than anything that a deep reading of Aristotle, Kant, and Mill could reasonably be expected to accomplish.

It is not surprising that such "read and talk" courses do little in themselves to produce students who actually care about and pursue justice. What may be more surprising is that many of the pedagogical antidotes designed to correct this deficiency are themselves shortsighted in significant ways, or so I shall argue. Service-learning courses, for example, are a step in the right direction because they take to heart the Aristotelian conviction that virtuous dispositions are habituated through practice rather than instilled by teaching. Yet most service-learning activities are not, by themselves, sufficient to address and counter the full range of preexisting dispositions that actively incline students away from the pursuit of justice.[3] Students do not come to service-learning courses as blank slates needing only to have brand-new dispositions instilled that were not present before. Instead, they are repositories of often well-established competing dispositions that may choke off the seedling dispositions toward justice that may otherwise be nurtured in service-learning activities. A pedagogical strategy without sufficient attention to these competing dispositions will likely diminish the prospects for transformation through service-learning. I hope to show that a more comprehensive dispositional formation could be advanced in service-learning courses by the inclusion of additional moral exercises based on several of the other traditional Christian spiritual disciplines.[4]

This paper will proceed in three parts. First, I will briefly recount my own experience conducting a service-learning course to further illustrate the nature of the problem I hope to address. Second, I will set out a portion of Immanuel Kant's doctrine of virtue that includes a significant model of dispositional formation. The title of this paper is taken from Kant's own claim that while dispositions cannot be considered virtues in themselves alone, they can nevertheless be cultivated and formed strategically in order to prepare the way for the development of virtue in general and justice in particular. In a final section, I hope to make this Kantian theoretical framework more concrete by setting out models of the spiritual disciplines from the writings of Thomas Merton for inspiration about how to shape and cultivate untamed dispositions holistically. I have chosen this monastic conception of the spiritual disciplines as my template for practical suggestions because of the long, successful tradition of taking broken humans and preparing their souls for an encounter with God. The parallels between the spiritual preparation Merton describes and the kind of preparation I think may be necessary for moral transformation to take hold suggest a robust slate of practices that could significantly enrich courses that hope ultimately to promote justice.

"Poverty and Wealth": An Exercise in Service-Learning

A short time ago I set out to explore the possibilities of transformational pedagogy by developing a service-learning version of a standard course offering, "Poverty and Wealth: Issues in Economic Justice." It was my hope that in the mix of philosophical argument, theological reflection, and face-to-face encounters with those experiencing poverty, my students would leave the course with more than a mere increase in awareness of the social problems and the range of moral arguments that address those problems. I hoped for changed people – living embodiments of a rooted and growing justice.[5]

During the semester students wrote journal entries chronicling the impact of the course and the service-learning experiences, and their personal reflections told an interesting story. Those who came into the class with a conviction that at least some forms of pervasive poverty are signs of deep structural injustice and who were open to changing their own actions accordingly left powerfully transformed by the course. On the other hand, those who came into the course apathetic about injustice almost universally left in that same state or worse, even after being met with extensive opportunities for character-shaping reflection and action. Neither the cognitive work nor the repeated service activities made much of a dent, at least in the short term.

I cannot hope to offer a complete analysis of this particular course's transformational success or failure, but the journals and classroom discussion did offer several clues that suggest a hypothesis worthy of exploration. Those who began the course without a strong incentive to develop dispositions toward justice often raised objections to our "do-gooding" that were *by their own admission* clearly motivated by several other preexisting dispositional incentives that ran contrary to or softened the desire for justice. Not surprisingly, the most common counter-dispositions had to do with deeply ingrained acquisitive desires and a profound sense of entitlement regarding possessions.[6] After reflecting on the course, it became clear to me that I had not done enough to address the richness and complexity of each student's dispositional set, or character, as a whole. I had hoped that simply through the practice and habituation of just actions through carefully crafted service-learning exercises, *all* rival dispositions would be confronted and diminished at a level commensurate with the regularity and power of the exercises themselves. What I came to realize is that there is no *single* contra-justice disposition that can be addressed therapeutically by rehearsing just actions.[7] Instead, the dispositions that counter the pursuit of justice are often quite varied and interconnected in such a way that a more comprehensive strategy will be required to establish the pedagogical and character-shaping conditions that can make a disposition toward justice take hold.

As a response to these considerations, it would seem that to invigorate the development of a disposition toward justice we should look for ways to habituate resistance to the interconnected matrix of dispositions that might counter this virtue. While service-learning will play an important role in this process, I will suggest that a thicker range of formational activities is required to produce a less obstructed path toward justice. In short, teachers who desire to "educate for justice" must think more carefully about how to "prepare the way for justice." In Immanuel Kant's *Metaphysics of Morals*, we find the rudiments of a conceptual framework that may be of some use in thinking about how to achieve this preparation.[8]

Kant on the Strategic Formation of Dispositions

If the strategic formation of dispositions is to play a priming or preparatory role in transformational moral education, it would seem that Kant would be an unlikely resource for the development of such a view. In Kantian jargon, inclinations are something like habitual desires, roughly equivalent to one species of the kind of dispositions that are of central concern in this paper.[9] Kant viewed the inclinational side of humanity with considerable suspicion, and he was quite explicitly opposed to any version of morality which suggested that virtue was completely achieved by the habituation of certain positive dispositions like sympathy, generosity, or even justice. Kant claimed that inclinations are at best *luckily* in harmony with duty, and at worst constantly standing as obstacles to pursuing our duty – that is, either entirely unreliable as sources of virtue, or things that must consistently be thwarted in order for virtue to take hold.[10] One need not look far to find examples of inclinations that run contrary to duty. Though perhaps harmless in itself, the common human tendency – hardened through practice and custom – to seek self-preservation when threatened can lead to disastrous moral consequences if undirected. And on the other end of the spectrum, an inclination toward the apparently morally valuable disposition of sympathy does not seem to point us universally in the direction of virtue. Barbara Herman gives the interesting example of a person whose carefully cultivated sympathetic reactions cause him or her to assist (in violation of a seemingly clear moral duty) a fleeing burglar who finds his burden a bit too much to handle.[11] In both types of situations, it seems that our inclinational side has led us astray, and as a result, at times, Kant speaks as though it would be better for us if the habitual passion-driven features of our humanity were cast aside once and for all.[12] So my appeal to Kant with respect to the strategic formation of dispositions as a key to successful moral education may seem a bit puzzling.

To avoid making this paper an exercise in Kantian exegesis, I will not attempt to recount in any detail the various ways sympathetic commentators have softened some of the perceived rougher edges of Kant's view.[13] It is enough to recognize that the *standard view* of Kant on the role of certain dispositional states in our moral agency draws almost exclusively from the relatively early *Grounding of the Metaphysics of Morals* and ignores an extensive body of Kant's own later works in moral philosophy. These later texts significantly enrich Kant's ability to enter into dialogue with moral thinkers who would more clearly be assigned the title "Virtue Ethicists."[14] I intend to draw from these later Kantian texts to illustrate the role that comprehensive dispositional formation may play in the service of transformational pedagogy.

Consider Kant's treatment of morally helpful dispositions such as sympathy. Kant claims that it is a duty to actively sympathize with those who are suffering, and "to this end it is therefore an indirect duty to cultivate the compassionate natural ... feelings in us, and to make use of them as so many means to sympathy based on moral principles and the feeling appropriate to them."[15] Over and against the received view, then, Kant claims that while the development of a disposition toward sympathy is not sufficient for virtue, it nevertheless plays an important role in moving virtue along. For the sake of clarity, we might call these dispositions "helping dispositions" because they provide a form of motivational surge or counterbalance which insure that the representation of one's duty (for Kant this is sufficient to motivate one to moral action)[16] will not be consistently overcome by terrifically strong counterincentives.[17] Helping dispositions act as an aid to the incentive of duty itself in those cases where the presence of strong counterincentives would otherwise tempt one to ignore the clear and sufficiently powerful call to duty.

The connection to my pedagogical questions should be clear, but perhaps in a rather obvious and unhelpful sort of way. Surely one of the goals of service-learning, for example, is to cultivate dispositions that offer this type of assistance to virtue, to help it along.[18] Kant admits as much when he claims that "it is ... a duty not to avoid the places where the poor who lack the most basic necessities are to be found but rather to seek them out, and not to shun sickrooms or debtors' prisons and so forth in order to avoid sharing painful feelings one may not be able to resist."[19] Using whatever means at our disposal, we should help our students develop dispositions to sympathy and justice so that the call to assist the marginalized will not be defeated by an onslaught of temptations and incentives to turn away. For those who already see the value in helping students to cultivate helping dispositions as part of a comprehensive moral education, the only real surprise here is that Kant, consistently represented as anti-inclination and overly infatuated with pure rationality, seems to be an ally in this conversation about dispositional formation.

At this point, however, I should draw attention once again to the central claim of this paper. Courses that only serve to develop such helping dispositions will likely fall short in the way that my own service-learning course fell short: by oversimplifying the dispositional set of each student and assuming that the cultivation of a helping disposition alone will sufficiently confront and overcome the diversity of incentives that run counter to justice. Kant's own writings contain the theoretical resources to suggest a broader strategy that involves undermining or resisting counterincentives rather than merely seeking to develop one powerful incentive toward justice which can rise above that oppositional fray. In what follows I will set out and show the pedagogical implications of this view.

In *The Metaphysics of Morals*, Kant tries to explain why he can legitimately embrace the common conviction that we ought to avoid the wanton destruction of inanimate objects of beauty. Many people share the belief that, in spite of the fact that beautiful crystal formations or alpine flowers cannot be harmed in the same way as humans, the mindless destruction of such inanimate objects seems *morally* troublesome. Since Kant's moral system is grounded in respect for *rational* nature, it would seem that such respect for inanimate, nonrational nature would find, at best, an *ad hoc* home. Nevertheless, Kant claims in a crucial passage that "a propensity to wanton destruction of what is beautiful in inanimate nature (*spiritus destructionis*) is opposed to a human being's duty to himself; for it weakens or uproots that feeling in him which, though not of itself moral, is still a disposition of sensibility that greatly promotes morality or at least prepares the way for it: the disposition, namely, to love something (e.g., beautiful crystal formations, the indescribable beauty of plants) even apart from any intention to use it."[20]

The exact justification and content of the duty to oneself that Kant specifies here are not as important for my purposes as another general insight offered in this text. In light of Kant's claim that some dispositions may *weaken or uproot others*, it becomes clear that the strategic development of some dispositions can help "prepare the way for morality" by doing battle with disruptive or even destructive tendencies in our inclinational structures. So I will add to the notion of a "helping disposition" the dual concepts of "uprooting" and "bulwark dispositions." Uprooting dispositions actually succeed in undermining a problematic disposition so successfully that it is no longer operative. Bulwark dispositions do not remove other dispositions entirely but instead offer a form of resistance that serves to ameliorate their impact. Both types of dispositions are used to achieve a kind of psychical level playing field in which troublesome human propensities are given a form of moral therapy through counterhabituation. When these particular kinds of dispositions are cultivated and employed, it is not to inspire or motivate some particular moral action as in the case of helping dispositions. Instead, these dispositions may serve to blunt the force of other inclinations which may consistently turn us away from duty.

The importance of uprooting and bulwark dispositions becomes clearer when we recognize the kinds of hardened character traits that render our moral powers impotent. In Kant's account of moral agency, we find at least three parts of our psychological makeup that could act as obstacles to the development of virtue: inclinations in general and two more specific subclasses of inclinations called passions and affects. As I have mentioned earlier, inclinations are habitual desires. In spite of the fact that Kant sometimes seems to suggest that we would do better to live entirely free of all inclinations,[21] the balance of the evidence suggests that inclinations as such are only problematic insofar as they obfuscate and challenge duty. Kant clearly states that the primary function of human inclinations is something like need-fulfillment, self-preservation, and happiness, so while they may run amok and carry us far beyond this initial purpose, their fundamental function is constructive.[22]

The two kinds of inclinations that *regularly* challenge moral development are passions and affects. Passions are inclinations that have become so hardened by intentional acceptance and habitual practice that they are no longer easily susceptible to constraint by reason.[23] As Kant puts it, a passion "is an enchantment that refuses to be corrected."[24] Affects, on the other hand, are impulsive and short-lived emotional responses to circumstance that interfere with our ability to deliberate carefully about what our appropriate response should be.[25] A flash of impulsive anger is an example of an affect, and if that anger is harbored, cultivated, and practiced, it could very well harden into the lasting passion of hatred. The affect of anger may preclude careful reflection, presumably the kind necessary to discern whether we may act in a particular way by assessing our maxim against the demands of fundamental moral principles (in Kant's case, the categorical imperative). The passion of hatred consistently and intentionally inclines one away from the requirements of duty. In both cases, virtue is undermined by the presence of these intractable inclinations. It seems clear that moral strength may be developed, in part, by finding ways to diminish the influence of such passions and affects. The strategic cultivation of helping, uprooting, and bulwark dispositions can serve this function well.

As one finds an entrenched passion, it may be that one of the most effective ways to keep it from inclining one away from one's moral duty is to engage in practices that will cultivate a bulwark disposition to provide balance and resistance. If a person discovers that he or she is eaten up with hatred of a particular person or group, the separate cultivation of a more general desire to build others up may take enough of the edge off the hatred for virtue to gain purchase. This passion that might otherwise divert one from moral excellence is then checked by other motivational forces.[26] Though the metaphor is far from perfect, the image of two evenly matched forces reaching a stalemate on the battlefield gives a snapshot of the model of the bulwark dispositions. In the space created by the stalemate, the seeds of virtue can begin to flourish.

A similar story could be told about the impulsive affects that momentarily blind individuals to the course of action that would and should be chosen given calm deliberation. If we take the affect of anger as our example, we have in mind those who are clouded in deliberation and action by flashes of temper. According to Kant, one who recognizes this problem upon introspection would do well to find some practice of life that replaces impulse with a coolness and patience befitting the sage. In other words, the development of the disposition of patience might well gradually uproot the tendency toward impulsive anger. Kant's own specific suggestion about how to address the affect of anger initially sounds odd, but at least it provides evidence that Kant was aware that affects had to be dealt with through counterhabituation. Kant claims that when one begins to experience impulsive anger, he or she should practice sitting down to begin the process of relaxation that might then soften the impact of the affect.[27] Perhaps routine practices of this kind might have a lasting impact on the impulse itself.

Though I have suggested a threefold division among helping, bulwark, and uprooting dispositions, there is nothing to rule out the possibility that one disposition may serve in two or more of those roles. For example, a sympathetic disposition acts in its helping role most clearly when one previously enjoyed no special attraction to sympathetic actions. But one might also have a morally charged and active counterincentive which directly pushes one away from sympathetic action – for example, one might actively dislike the person who is nevertheless worthy of sympathetic treatment. In the former case, one experiences no powerful pull in the direction of sympathy; in the latter case, one is actively pulled away from sympathy. In the latter case, sympathy may provide a necessary bulwark that resists the counterincentive in addition to its role as a helping disposition. So in some cases the development of a single disposition can address multiple problematic aspects of a person's overall character.

This multitasking characteristic of some dispositions would explain why the development of a sense of and interest in justice through service-learning exercises can be transformative by itself for some students. Surely some students will find that their most troublesome dispositions are softened through the affective changes wrought by service-learning activities alone, but I still would like to suggest that this would be a fortuitous event rather than a necessary outcome. It seems that the better path is to develop purposeful ways to address a broader swath of the student's dispositional set rather than hoping that the development of a service-learning component will do all the work necessary.

We would do well to note that the dispositions which prepare the way for morality must not themselves be cultivated into affects and passions that are then also resistant to future circumstances where morality would dictate that they not be heeded. Instead, we seek a kind of "moral apathy" championed by Kant that issues in a tranquil mind, one that has achieved a kind of psychic balance with the way cleared for duty to engage our respect.[28] Such apathy presupposes no attempt to extirpate any and all emotion. This is no call to pure detachment commonly associated with some interpretations (often mistaken) of Stoicism.[29] Instead, there is merely a form of balance with respect to the emotions and desires that keeps them from clouding or overpowering the incentive of duty. So the training we can do in the pursuit of moral perfection is not simply about training good inclinations to replace bad ones. Instead, we are clearing space for careful moral deliberation and judgment, thereby becoming ever more attuned to the regulative principle at the heart of morality, whatever it may be. We are developing a better awareness of morality's call such that temptations from inclination hold less sway.

Though most of the practical implications of this view will not be addressed until the final section of this paper, its basic significance for pedagogy should be clear. In addition to thinking about ways to develop dispositions that prompt direct actions of compassion, justice, or the other cardinal virtues, teachers should also seek to target and minimize other justice-thwarting dispositions. The more we begin to think about how we can achieve the kind of psychic balance described by Kant, the greater the hope will be that even those who come in to a course with significant dispositional obstacles will at least see the beginnings of the changes that would make their lives fertile for a subsequent birth of justice.

Where do we look for models that will help us think about how to effectively carry out dispositional formation of the sort I have been describing? I will suggest in the final section of my paper that the exercise of spiritual disciplines (or perhaps secular analogues, should the educational context require it) will best achieve the dispositional transformation we desire.

The Spiritual Disciplines as Formational Model and Authentic Practice

While exploring the role that Christian spirituality can play in a broadened conception of moral transformation, I will consider spirituality rather narrowly as the practice of spiritual disciplines (e.g., prayer, fasting, meditation and the like) aimed at the dual targets of a more complete union with God and a life that more clearly reflects the values of the kingdom of God. Since these types of spiritual disciplines are widely practiced and in disparate ways, I will narrow my focus even more to include only the spiritual practices of Trappist monasticism in general and Thomas Merton in particular. I am limiting the concept of spirituality in this way not because I assume that Merton's form of monastic spirituality is the only or even the ideal form of spirituality but because I think that the practice of the spiritual disciplines in that context most closely parallels the kind of dispositional formation I have in mind for moral education.

Spiritual practices of this sort are relevant to transformational pedagogy in two possible ways. First, the practice of the spiritual disciplines themselves provides a centuries-old analogical model for the kind of habituation that can cultivate some dispositions or diminish the influence of others. The fact that my proposal requires teachers to take the student's broader dispositional set into account in configuring active learning exercises seems to necessitate a nearly impossible task. How will we know the dispositional set of each student well enough to craft individual exercises that will effectively prepare the way for justice? The spiritual disciplines act as a shorthand summary of the Christian tradition's understanding of the kinds of dispositions endemic to the human condition itself that might need pruning and shaping to clear the way for a person's regular encounter with God. Since I believe that the same negative proclivities will likely act as barriers to the person's interest in and pursuit of justice, the disciplines also provide a comprehensive model for disposition formation to clear the way for justice. Second, in institutional contexts that can sustain a more confessional approach in the classroom, the actual practice of the spiritual disciplines in their thickest transcendent sense allows for a genuine encounter with the transforming Spirit of Christ, and this in turn should provide a far greater preparation for justice than the practice of disciplines that are "spiritual" in name only. In what follows, I will explain how the spiritual disciplines could be used as models for moral formation, and at the end of my paper I will more briefly address the prospects for more authentic practices of spirituality.

In *The Silent Life*, Merton claims that "Monastic solitude, poverty, obedience, silence, and prayer dispose the soul for [its] mysterious destiny in God. Asceticism itself does not produce divine union as its direct result. It only disposes the soul for union. The various practices of monastic asceticism are more or less valuable to the monk in proportion as they help him to accomplish the inner and spiritual work that needs to be done to make his soul poor, and humble, and empty, in the mystery of the presence of God."[30] In *Life and Holiness* he claims that "our seeking of God is not all a matter of our finding him by means of certain ascetic techniques. It is rather a quieting and ordering of our whole life by self-denial, prayer, and good works, so that God himself, who seeks us more than we seek him, can 'find us' and 'take possession of us.'"[31] What Merton makes clear in both passages is that our spiritual action is a form of soul preparation. It is not an end in itself, and the work of divine union is God's action, not the direct result of some purely human action.

What I have been suggesting thus far is that the training and shaping of our dispositions will not constitute the realization of moral transformation in the final sense, but it will provide an essential step in that direction by disposing the soul for a more ready and fruitful encounter with the moral call for justice. The analogy with the work of the spiritual disciplines in disposing the soul for union with God is useful, because in both cases the soul must be prepared either by cultivating dispositions that will incline us to more self-denial and openness toward the other or by pruning dispositions that incline us to the reverse.[32]

We can make the parallels between spiritual practices and the kind of dispositional work I have been describing more lively by leaving the realm of the abstract and moving toward specific concrete examples. Let us consider a particular passion that commonly obstructs many students' pursuit of social justice.[33] In Plato's *Republic* Socrates makes it clear that before justice would be widespread, human beings would have to confront any deeply ingrained desire to "outdo others" – to seek more than their share. This negative disposition is called *pleonexia*.[34] Leaving aside for now the complicated questions about what constitutes a legitimate share of the basic goods of society and the other substantive questions about justice, I would suggest that consumer culture has bequeathed a legacy of acquisitiveness and competitiveness to many students, which at its limit looks very much like *pleonexia*.[35] Many affluent societies have taken it as an article of economic faith that acquisitiveness has no legitimate upper bound, and as the student journal entries from my course demonstrated, for many students this translates into a profound sense of both aspiration and entitlement. There is very little recognition that what it is possible to achieve may not actually be consistent with a just social order. Many are startled and even angered by Aquinas' suggestion in the *Summa* that what we have in abundance belongs to the poor by right.[36] The drive to acquire and outdo is alive and well, and as a result justice is often undervalued and undermined.[37]

In light of the specific hurdle presented by *pleonexia*, those interested in helping students move toward habits of just actions will likely employ a matrix of pedagogical strategies. Some progress may be made simply by introducing students to theories of justice that set out alternative conceptions of one's legitimate share relative to others. This is the kind of cognitive transformation that I believe lives at the heart of all valuable ethics courses whether concerned with overall moral transformation or not.[38] In addition, pleonexia may be addressed directly by an attempt through service-learning and similar experiences to habituate something like a helping disposition to seek out and establish justice. But that direct approach would be significantly buttressed by an appeal to the kind of strategic dispositional formation I have been touting. It seems that if one were to present the student with opportunities to set up bulwark dispositions that counter the *pleonexia* in a more indirect way, any helping dispositions that would steer someone toward justice would face a clearer path.

The spiritual discipline of poverty, or voluntary simplicity as I shall call it, could provide the model for the development of a successful bulwark disposition against various levels of *pleonexia*. The practice of relinquishing hold of one's physical possessions is worth nothing in itself. Instead, the inner transformations of attitude and tendency gained through the outward practice provide its warrant. Merton notes that some monks "obligate themselves to be poor, chaste, and obedient, thereby renouncing their own wills, denying themselves, and liberating themselves from mundane attachments in order to give themselves even more perfectly to Christ."[39] As this passage indicates, simplicity (and chastity and obedience as well) expressed as a spiritual discipline is first and foremost an attempt to clear away things that clutter both our inner and outer lives, allowing for a sharper focus upon God alone. But the practice is also justified by the ways in which it teaches the soul about healthy detachment from a pervasive and alluring temporality and about the falsehood of any individualistic myths we espouse about self-sufficiency. The shedding of items about which we care deeply can help to remind us of how frequently *things own us* and how frequently we trick ourselves into believing that as long as we have our things, we need little else.

Recall that this discipline is not designed to cultivate justice in itself. An appropriate level of detachment from one's possessions and recognition of relationships of mutual dependence rather than self-sufficiency could blunt the force of the common streams of acquisitiveness without ever making specific reference to questions about whether others have a legitimate claim upon some of one's abundance. In short, it may be useful to begin helping students to pry their own fingers from their possessions long before they ever have to think about making sacrifices of those things to address unjust inequities in society. The by-product, however, will be that thinking about justice subsequently will be less encumbered by *pleonexia*. In a short chapter about the disposition of detachment, Merton explains that "when you love and desire things for their own sakes, even though you may understand general moral principles, you do not know how to apply them."[40] Without their eyes clouded by a love for things, students may more easily be able to see the moral significance of others' need for things.

The obvious question that follows this kind of recommendation will likely be, How does a teacher introduce the discipline of voluntary simplicity in a classroom context? How can this kind of bulwark disposition be cultivated? The practice of renunciation associated with the spiritual discipline of voluntary simplicity can at least be approximated in some limited ways. Typical syllabus requirements could include a section of assignments called "moral exercises," and students could choose from a bank of long- and short-term practices that will be assessed as a part of a journal requirement for the whole term. With respect to voluntary simplicity, the possible practices are relatively straightforward. One option would require that the student give up for at least the duration of the term and preferably longer some object or practice that has either aesthetic, sentimental, or instrumental significance to him or her (a cell phone, a vehicle, weekly shopping sprees, or similar items). Over the course of the term, the student would be asked to reflect in written form on a series of questions posed by the instructor about the experience of willfully disengaging from something of subjective importance. For those who adjust quickly to the absence, further reductions could be suggested. For those who take on the greatest challenges, (e.g., those who do without their car for at least a term) it seems reasonable to expect some development of a disposition of detachment and perhaps a dampening of the impulse toward *pleonexia*. Students who engage in one exercise in one semester will neither be true practitioners of the simple life nor freed entirely from the excessive impulse toward *pleonexia*. Nevertheless, I remain convinced that any progress in constructive dispositional development and psychical balance makes for a significantly improved course in moral philosophy and opens the door wider to the hoped-for march toward true justice.[41]

Thus far, I have been using spiritual disciplines as a model for a sort of moral gymnastics to help students address dispositional imbalances that could consistently turn them aside from moral duty. In this sense, they are hardly worthy of the name *"spiritual* disciplines," because there is no real sense of the transcendent purpose and value of the disciplines themselves.[42] What I have described is a mere shadow of what could be. The reason I have characterized them in this seemingly impoverished way first is that not all of the people who might be interested in dispositional formation as a pedagogical method teach in contexts that can sustain a more direct appeal to theological considerations. Furthermore, I have been arguing that in such cases, the kind of moral gymnastics described above can offer significant advantages over typical service-learning courses with respect to the overall formation of the students. Finally, the classroom is not a closed context. Even when the teacher him- or herself is not highlighting a specifically transcendent component, those students who are otherwise engaged in spiritual activity outside the class could import their own transcendent component and experience the analogues to the spiritual disciplines in their fullness.[43] So I would like to suggest that even the shadow of the spiritual disciplines can bear great fruit.

Nevertheless, those who teach in institutions with an intentional confessional stance may find opportunity to employ the spiritual disciplines in their thicker sense, further empowering the students' fledgling march toward justice. In what remains, I will make some suggestions about what could be added by an intentionally "spiritual" component. The spiritual disciplines all are meant to open up possibilities for deeper union with God, but this is not necessarily separate from another role of the disciplines – furthering the soul's lifelong march toward moral holiness and toward the realization of God's kingdom on earth. It is clear from Merton's writings that human attempts to change the world are empty without an infusion of the Spirit in the activist's life. "An activity that is based on the frenzies and impulsions of human ambition is a delusion and an obstacle to grace. It gets in the way of God's will, and it creates more problems than it solves. We must learn to distinguish between the pseudo spirituality of activism and the true vitality and energy of Christian action guided by the Spirit."[44] It seems reasonable (though perhaps also controversial) to believe that no matter where genuine injustice is opposed, we see the Spirit of Christ in action, but in light of the complexities of injustice itself and its causes and conditions in real world situations, and more importantly in light of the complex motivations that cause us to seek what we believe best represents justice, we would do well to forestall purely human endeavors robbed of the vitality and energy of the Spirit's direction. Perhaps the best way to insure that our strategic cultivation of dispositions will amount to more than frivolous human frenzies is, when possible in our educational contexts, not to simply model our moral formation after the spiritual disciplines but to actually practice them.

Putting the "spirit" back into the spiritual disciplines can also help remove another obstacle to the pursuit of justice. Earlier I suggested that one of the other reasons students may resist the steadfast commitment to justice is that the scope of the injustice in the world makes all efforts to alleviate it seem futile. This sense of futility is perhaps best expressed as an affect, because it manifests as a burst of dark emotion which can forestall right action. As one of my students put it out of genuine exasperation and later depression, "Where would I even think about starting to address something so overwhelming?" But one of the specific outcomes of spiritual practice is a disposition that may not have a realistic expression in a non-religious context. Paul lists the three great virtues in Corinthians. Alongside faith and love, we find hope. It is a central Christian conviction that though the kingdom has come, it is yet coming, and students may find the resources in the practice of authentic spiritual disciplines to challenge apathy and paralysis in the hope of its coming.[45]

Finally, the practice of the spiritual disciplines in their thick sense can develop the moral imagination necessary to break out of our narrow and limited perspectives about how the world operates and what people are like. A pithy statement of the purpose of the disciplines, particularly the contemplative practices, is to obtain the "vision of God." But this statement of purpose contains a fruitful ambiguity, because we not only want to be able to contemplate God's character, love, and grace in the midst of our spiritual practices; we also want the infusion of God's spirit to transform our own vision of humanity and the world. One gets a sense of how different this world can look when we read Merton's account of a mundane moment when "the special clumsy beauty of this particular colt on this April day in this field under these clouds is a holiness consecrated to God by his own creative wisdom [declaring] the glory of God."[46] We not only want to see God, we want to see as God sees and value as God values. When we see as God sees, victims of an unjust social order are not simply dismissed as warranting their own miseries through lack of effort and initiative. When we see as God sees, we understand that humanity, all of it, is created a little lower than the angels and warrants our respect, our attention, and our care. When we see as God sees, the downtrodden least of these melt away to reveal the face of Christ. The authentic practice of the disciplines can grant us this vision.

Conclusion

I have been arguing that common attempts at the promotion of justice in moral education can suffer from a certain narrowness of vision. In many instances, students quite simply are not morally prepared to make the gargantuan leap from often sheltered and privileged lives to the sacrificial steps required to stand up and support the rights of all, especially the oppressed. Tossing such students into situations where they must go through the motions of justice will not likely bear much fruit unless the ground of their dispositional set is being carefully tilled as well. I hope to have shown that such tilling can be accomplished by adopting the spiritual disciplines as a way to form helping, bulwark, and uprooting dispositions that can then serve to clear a path toward justice. As instructors we cannot guarantee that someone will take the project of morality seriously enough to turn whatever moral exercises we may offer into a fully lived-out justice. But if we grant that transformational moral education is a worthwhile goal, we are at least responsible for creating the conditions under which justice may be cultivated with as little resistance as possible.

Notes

1   I would like to thank the participants of the "Spirituality, Justice, and Pedagogy" conference who offered comments after a presentation of an earlier version of this article. I would also like to thank anonymous reviewers who have offered important suggestions that ultimately helped to clarify and (I hope) strengthen my view.

2   I acknowledge that the idea that an ethics class could or should be about "moral formation and transformation" is controversial in itself. I have reservations about this idea myself, but for the purposes of this paper I will simply take it for granted (without argument) that at least one possible objective of moral education, particularly at schools with a confessional religious bent, is to produce better, more virtuous people.

3   Service-learning activities are complex affairs, and because the exact nature of the eventual experience is unknown and the various cognitive and affective situations of each learner will often dictate how that experience is received, their transformative value is rarely envisioned completely by the planner. Sometimes students come into a course well primed, and the service-learning experience provides the perfect fuel for the transformation engine, but at least as frequently there are students with dispositional obstacles that are not as susceptible to reformation through service-learning activities. I defend a strategy that I believe will leave less to chance.

4   I should note that I will be developing this line of argument from the perspective of a moral philosopher and theologian as opposed to someone

engaged in social-scientific exploration. However, the construct I offer below could possibly illuminate pathways for future empirical research.

5   I will avoid setting out any substantive conception of justice in this paper, because I believe that the framework of moral formation I recommend is compatible with a number of competing conceptions of justice. I should acknowledge, however, that when I use the term *justice* throughout the paper, I have "distributive" justice in mind because distributive justice was the subject of my service-learning course. I am operating on the assumption that justice can require some level of assistance for those who experience significant poverty. Those who believe that justice never requires one to assist another in the absence of contracts or calls for reparations (certain libertarian views of justice might be described in this way) will likely reject my entire course project.

6   By "dispositions" I mean settled patterns of desire, emotion, attitude, or behavior, the collection of which forms the character of the individual. For a more complete account of dispositions and the role they play in moral formation and action, see Wolterstorff, Nicholas, *Educating for Responsible Action* (Grand Rapids, MI: Eerdmans, 1980) pp. 3-6.

7   One might argue that there is indeed a single contra-justice disposition: the vice of injustice. But merely identifying the oppositional term that labels the corresponding vice oversimplifies the problem in just the way I have described. Surely people who intentionally take what is not theirs or practice oppression as a matter of course would be able to address their vicious dispositions through repeated actions to the contrary, but most who fail to be just are not easily characterized by the presence of a disposition to injustice. Especially in the realm of economic justice, where justice is often satisfied with positive actions rather than mere noninterference, the dispositions which lead to inaction are varied and numerous.

8   I do not intend to offer a systematic treatment of Kant's stated view on moral education. I will instead develop a picture of moral formation that has Kantian elements in it. For a more systematic treatment of Kant's view of moral education, specifically as it relates to service-learning and spirituality, see Hare, John E., "Kantian Moral Education and Service-Learning" in Hefner, G. G. and C. D. Beversluis (eds.), *Commitment and Connection: Service-Learning and Christian Higher Education* (Lanham, MD: Univ. Press of America, 2002) pp. 73-96.

9   At the risk of some imprecision, I will use the terms *inclination* and *disposition* interchangeably.

10   Kant, Immanuel, *Grounding for the Metaphysics of Morals*, 3rd ed., trans. James W. Ellington (Indianapolis, IN: Hackett Publ., 1993) pp. 397-399. Following a common convention in Kantian scholarship, the page numbers will correspond to *Kant's gesammelte Schriften*, herausgegeben von

der Königlichen Preussischen Akademie der Wissenschaften, 23 volumes (Berlin: Walter de Gruyter, 1902).

11   Herman, Barbara, *The Practice of Moral Judgment* (Cambridge, MA: Harvard Univ. Press, 1993) pp. 4-5.

12   Kant (1993) pp. 398, 428.

13   Two important examples of the commentators doing this kind of work are Sherman, Nancy, *Making a Necessity of Virtue: Aristotle and Kant on Virtue* (Cambridge: Cambridge Univ. Press, 1997) and Baron, Marcia, *Kantian Ethics Almost Without Apology* (Ithaca, NY: Cornell Univ. Press, 1995).

14   I should also note that one need not be a Kantian to find the account of dispositional formation set out below appealing. One may, for example, adopt a different fundamental principle of morality from Kant's and still assume that dispositions should be formed in a way to clear the path for the consistent application of that principle. In addition, those who believe that morality is primarily about character and not principles may question whether this aspect of Kant's view is consistent with his emphasis upon universal principles, but I believe that they could and should still welcome his recognition that a person's character plays a significant role in the moral life.

15   Kant, Immanuel, *The Metaphysics of Morals*, ed. and trans. Mary Gregor (Cambridge: Cambridge Univ. Press, 1996) p. 457.

16   One of Kant's core doctrinal commitments is that the representation of duty provides its own sufficient incentive to be moral. I am not claiming, then, that the helping dispositions are meant to bridge any gap in duty's ability to motivate. Instead, the helping dispositions may simply act to ameliorate some of the temptations that would otherwise make it difficult for the incentive of duty to be most forcefully represented.

17   Henry Allison's account of this aspect of Kant's view is illuminating. See Allison, Henry E., *Kant's Theory of Freedom* (Cambridge: Cambridge Univ. Press, 1990) p. 167. Nancy Sherman labels Kant's doctrine of virtue a "structured composite" involving elements of both the affective and cognitive life. On her account, inclinations in the virtuous person are not to be dismissed but "conditioned and transformed" in the service of the broader desire to consistently act on moral principle. See Sherman (1997) p. 158.

18   I offer here no particular mechanism by which service-learning or the disciplines I will describe below accomplish disposition formation or transformation. However, Nicholas Wolterstorff has suggested a number of pedagogical factors that are known to influence human dispositions: (1) cognitive illumination sometimes gives us new *reasons* to act that are sufficient to dispose us to act, (2) *discipline* helps to attach appropriate positive or negative consequences to actions, which can then dispose us to act, (3)

modeling behavior can often inspire students to replicate that behavior, and (4) being in contact with those who suffer can draw out *empathy*, which in turn can dispose us to take up the cause of the oppressed. Though I suspect the practices of service-learning and other active learning strategies involve more than these four dimensions in terms of shaping dispositions (in particular some form of cognitively informed habituation to reinforce and stabilize the more straightforwardly cognitive elements listed above), each of these dimensions is nevertheless likely *part* of the explanation of why such strategies are successful. See Wolterstorff, Nicholas, "Teaching for Justice: On Shaping How Students Are Disposed to Act" in Joldersma, Clarence W. & Gloria Goris Stronks (eds.), *Educating for Shalom: Essays on Christian Higher Education* (Grand Rapids, MI: Eerdmans, 2004) pp. 148-152.

19   Kant (1996) p. 457.

20   Kant (1996) p. 443. He continues this line of thought with respect to our treatment of animals, claiming that "with regard to the animate but non-rational part of creation, violent and cruel treatment of animals is far more intimately opposed to a human being's duty to himself, and he has a duty to refrain from this; for it dulls his shared feeling of their suffering and so weakens and gradually uproots a natural predisposition that is very serviceable to morality in one's relations with other men."

21   Kant (1993) pp. 398, 428.

22   Kant, Immanuel, *Religion Within the Boundaries of Mere Reason*, ed. and trans. Allen Wood and George di Giovanni (Cambridge: Cambridge Univ. Press, 1998) p. 78; 58.

23   Kant (1996) p. 408.

24   Kant, Immanuel, *Anthropology from a Pragmatic Point of View*, trans. Victor Lyle Dowdell (Carbondale, IL: Southern Illinois Univ. Press, 1978) p. 266.

25   Kant (1996) p. 407.

26   I need to reiterate, however, that the counter forces do not, in themselves, constitute virtue. Instead, they are merely the preconditions of virtue because they prevent one's most deeply rooted temptations from consistently thwarting right action. As a reminder, the reason this does not constitute virtue in the Kantian schema is that the "building up" disposition is blind without being directed by moral principle. Virtue is achieved when one exhibits strength in performing one's duty (and it is not always one's duty to build others up).

27   Kant (1978) p. 252.

28   Kant (1996) pp. 408-409. Kant's use of the phrase "moral apathy" is indicative of the Stoic influence on his moral philosophy, so the term *apathy* should not be interpreted in the contemporary sense of the word.

Apathy is not indifference to emotion, but freedom from binding forces of passion.

29   Sherman (1997) p. 155.

30   Merton, Thomas, *The Silent Life* (New York: Farrar, Straus, and Giroux, 1957) pp. 3-4.

31   Merton, Thomas, *Life and Holiness* (New York: Image Books, 1963) p. 29.

32   The analogy could be extended on the supposition that *the possession of virtue* stands at the same mysterious junction of God's gift and human agency as *union with God*. If, as John E. Hare suggests, virtue really is the result of divine gift (though a gift thoroughly intertwined with some role for human willing and action), perhaps the most we can do is to "prepare the way." For more on the idea of virtue as mysterious divine gift, see Hare (2002) p. 77.

33   While I have suggested that the spiritual disciplines themselves provide a shorthand way of determining the general kinds of dispositions that may act as a barrier to both union with God and a life of justice, I believe that part of a detailed pedagogical strategy based on these basic ideas necessitates a more precise account of the kinds of specific affects and passions that seem to most commonly thwart our students' justice impulses. I will not engage in armchair psychology in the hopes of characterizing common dispositional situations of actual students, but I do not believe that in the absence of direct empirical study of students' psychologies we are helpless to say something about the propensities that are the most intractable. My specific examples in this paper have been chosen with reference to the anecdotal evidence gathered from student journals, and I have also been deeply influenced by various critics of consumer culture who illustrate how that particular culture works its way into settled patterns of consciousness, belief, and behavior. Several recent anthologies have emerged, and many make explicit reference to the kind of character that is groomed in consumer culture. See, e.g., Crocker, David & Toby Linden (eds.), *Ethics of Consumption: The Good Life, Justice, and Global Stewardship* (Lanham, MD: Rowman and Littlefield Publ., 1998); Doherty, Daniel & Amitai Etzioni (eds.), *Voluntary Simplicity: Responding to Consumer Culture* (Lanham, MD: Rowman and Littlefield Publ., 2003); and Schor, Juliet B. & Douglas B. Holt (eds.), *The Consumer Society Reader* (New York: The New Press, 2000). To develop the core ideas of my paper into a concrete proposal for curriculum and moral exercises, perhaps more precise research is warranted.

34   Plato mentions *pleonexia* as one of the key causes of injustice in the *Republic*. See Plato, *Republic*, 2nd ed., trans. G. M. A. Grube (Indianapolis, IN: Hackett Publ., 1992) p. 359c.

35   The exact definition of *pleonexia* as used by Plato is of secondary importance here. I am most interested in finding a convenient term that
describes to some degree a deep-seated disposition of competition and
acquisitiveness. If the choice of *pleonexia* is not quite true to Plato's intention, it may nevertheless be considered a term of art expressing the sense
that I have given it above.

36   Aquinas, *Summa Theologica*, II-II, Question 66, Article 7, in A. P.
d'Entreves (ed.), *Aquinas, Selected Political Writings*, trans. J. G. Dawson
(Oxford: Oxford Univ. Press, 1948) p. 171.

37   I certainly do not intend to suggest by my remarks that some passion like
pleonexia acts as a self-sufficient explanation of a student's failure to take
justice as a serious commitment. As I have stated, a comprehensive transformational pedagogy would have to countenance a number of possible
barriers, some dispositional and some not. In addition to the motivational
forces that act as obstacles, students may also lack a solid grasp of the
nature or significance of justice, or they may be paralyzed by the thought
that justice seems unattainable in light of the scope of the social problems
we face. These and other kinds of obstacles would have to be addressed
in their own right, but for the sake of clarity and simplicity I will focus here
on only one example of an intruding passion.

38   As I noted in footnote 18 above, Nicholas Wolterstorff believes such cognitive transformations may sometimes be sufficient to transform dispositions as well. The "matrix of pedagogical strategies" to which I refer above
should certainly include a variety of learning activities that concretize
Wolterstorff's schema of disposition influence (reasons, discipline, modeling, and empathy), especially when some aspect of that schema is not
already implicated in the service-learning activities and disciplines I recommend here. Wolterstorff (2004) pp. 148-152.

39   Merton (1963) p. 13.

40   Merton, Thomas, *New Seeds of Contemplation* (New York: New
Directions Books, 1962) p. 203.

41   I have only developed one example in this paper, but it is not for lack of
others. All of the spiritual disciplines, when exercised, consistently target
certain aspects of troublesome human dispositions, and so we could
develop a catalog of "moral exercises" that spring from knowledge about
how each discipline shapes character and prepares the soul for commun-
ion with God. It would admittedly be difficult to include and manage the
full catalog of exercises within the confines of one course, but since the
counterproductive dispositions in need of attention will likely fall under
general categories (like *pleonexia*) that may be ranked in terms of the
influence they exert on typical students, perhaps two or three exercises that
treat these main contenders can be developed and employed.

42 John E. Hare argues that because virtue comes as a "divine gift," we should keep moral education always "receptive to God's role in human morality." On the importance of keeping service-learning experiences in touch with the transcendent or "vertical" theme, see Hare (2002) pp. 74, 80-81, 85-90.

43 I am very grateful for the comments of an anonymous reviewer that helped me to see this point.

44 Merton (1963) pp. 8-9.

45 Cf. Wolterstorff (2004) pp. 153-154.

46 Merton (1962) p. 30.

Bibliography

Allison, Henry E., *Kant's Theory of Freedom* (Cambridge: Cambridge Univ. Press, 1990).

Aristotle, *Nicomachean Ethics*, trans. Terence Irwin, 2nd ed. (Indianapolis, IN: Hackett Publ., 1999).

Baron, Marcia, *Kantian Ethics Almost Without Apology* (Ithaca, NY: Cornell Univ. Press, 1995).

Crocker, David & Toby Linden (eds.), *Ethics of Consumption: The Good Life, Justice, and Global Stewardship* (Lanham, MD: Rowman and Littlefield Publ., 1998).

Doherty, Daniel & Amitai Etzioni (eds.), *Voluntary Simplicity: Responding to Consumer Culture* (Lanham, MD: Rowman and Littlefield Publ., 2003).

Hare, John E., "Kantian Morality and Service-Learning" in Hefner, G. G. and C. D. Beversluis (eds.), *Commitment and Connection: Service-Learning and Christian Higher Education* (Lanham, MD: Univ. Press of America, 2002), pp. 73-96.

Herman, Barbara, *The Practice of Moral Judgment* (Cambridge, MA: Harvard Univ. Press, 1993).

Kant, Immanuel, *Anthropology from a Pragmatic Point of View*, trans. Victor Lyle Dowdell (Carbondale, IL: Southern Illinois Univ. Press, 1978).

Kant, Immanuel, *Grounding for the Metaphysics of Morals*, 3rd ed., trans. James W. Ellington (Indianapolis, IN: Hackett Publ., 1993).

Kant, Immanuel, *The Metaphysics of Morals*, ed. and trans. Mary Gregor (Cambridge: Cambridge Univ. Press, 1996).

Kant, Immanuel, *Religion Within the Boundaries of Mere Reason*, ed. and trans. Allen Wood and George di Giovanni (Cambridge: Cambridge Univ. Press, 1998).

Merton, Thomas, *The Silent Life* (New York: Farrar, Straus, and Giroux, 1957).

Merton, Thomas, *New Seeds of Contemplation* (New York: New Directions Books, 1962).

Merton, Thomas, *Life and Holiness* (New York: Image Books, 1963).

Plato, *Republic*, trans. G. M. A. Grube, 2nd ed. (Indianapolis, IN: Hackett Publ., Inc., 1992).

Schor, Juliet B. & Douglas B. Holt (eds.), *The Consumer Society Reader* (New York: The New Press, 2000).

Sherman, Nancy, *Making a Necessity of Virtue: Aristotle and Kant on Virtue* (Cambridge: Cambridge Univ. Press, 1997).

Wolterstorff, Nicholas, *Educating for Responsible Action* (Grand Rapids, MI: Eerdmans, 1980).

Wolterstorff, Nicholas, "Teaching for Justice: On Shaping How Students Are Disposed to Act" in Joldersma, Clarence W. & Gloria Goris Stronks (eds.), *Educating for Shalom: Essays on Christian Higher Education* (Grand Rapids, MI: Eerdmans, 2004) pp. 135-154.

Journal of Education & Christian Belief

Editors: John Shortt, David I. Smith, and John Sullivan

Concerned with current educational thinking from a Christian perspective

Instructions to Contributors

EDITORIAL ADDRESSES:

USA and Canada:

Dr. David Smith,
JE&CB Editor
The Kuyers Institute,
Calvin College
3201 Burton Street SE
Grand Rapids, MI 49546
USA
Tel: +1 (616) 526-8609
Fax: +1 (616) 526-8583
E-mail: jecb@calvin.edu

Dr. Jan Gormas,
JE&CB Reviews Editor
Education Department,
Calvin College
3201 Burton Street SE
Grand Rapids, MI 49546
USA
Tel: +1 (616) 526-6286
Fax: +1 (616) 526-6505
E-mail: jecb@calvin.edu

UK and Rest of World:

Dr. John Shortt, JE&CB Editor
1 Kiteleys Green
Leighton Buzzard, Beds.
LU7 3LD, UK
Tel: +44 1525 379709
Fax: +44 870 1372902
E-mail:editor@jecb.org
E-mail: reviews@jecb.org

ARTICLES:

Manuscripts for publication and other editorial correspondence should be addressed to either Dr. David Smith (USA and Canada) or Dr. John Shortt (UK and Rest of World) at the appropriate address above.

Manuscripts should be typewritten or computer printed with wide margins. Everything, including notes, should be double-spaced. A note of the number of words in the article, although not essential, is helpful. Contributors should submit copy in a file attached to an e-mail or on diskette. To facilitate anonymous review by referees, the author's name should appear only on a detachable title page. Contributors should retain copies of their manuscripts and computer files since the editors can take no responsibility in case of loss or damage.

Abstract: The manuscript should be accompanied by an abstract of 100 words or less and a list of key words and phrases that could be used to index the article.

References: All references should be numbered consecutively in the text. The notes themselves, which are to contain where appropriate full bibliographic data, should be typed onto a separate sheet at the end of the article. Contributors should follow the format for references and bibliographies used in the journal.

Author Affiliation: A note of the author's position in not more than 25 words should be included at the end of the manuscript.

BOOK REVIEWS:

Books for review should be sent to either Dr. Jan Gormas (USA and Canada) or Dr. John Shortt (UK and Rest of World) at the addresses above. Full instructions to reviewers will be sent together with books for review.

The editors normally solicit book reviews from members of a panel of reviewers. Those who wish to be considered for this panel are invited to write with some detail of their suitability and background.

Suggestions are welcome from readers regarding books that they consider should be reviewed in the journal.

Current Subscription Rates		
	Period	
	One Year	Two/Three Years, per Year
Institutions		
UK and western Europe	£24.10	£22.10
North America	$62.75 (U.S.)	$56.50 (U.S.)
Elsewhere	£25.10	£22.60
Individuals		
UK and western Europe	£24.10	£22.10
North America	$41.40 (U.S.)	$37.30 (U.S.)
Elsewhere	£25.10	£22.60

2/3rds world, individuals and institutions:
50% discount on the overseas sterling (£) rates listed above
All subscriptions to:
The Stapleford Centre, The Old Lace Mill, Frederick Road,
Stapleford, Nottingham NG9 8FN, UK
Tel: +44 (0) 115 939 6270; Fax: +44 (0) 115 939 2076; Email: subs@jecb.org
Secure online payment of subscriptions by credit card is available at www.jecb.org
Please quote your Subscription Reference Number in all correspondence.
This appears on the address label used to send your copies to you.